History Riddles

A Treasure Trove Book

History Riddles

A Treasure Trove Book

Leon Conrad

Winchester, UK
Washington, USA

First published by Liberalis Books, 2015
Liberalis Books is an imprint of John Hunt Publishing Ltd., Laurel House, Station Approach, Alresford, Hants, SO24 9JH, UK
office1@jhpbooks.net
www.liberalisbooks.com

For distributor details and how to order please visit the 'Ordering' section on our website.

ISBN: 978 1 78279 294 9

A CIP catalogue record for this book is available from the British Library.

Design: Lee Nash

Printed in the USA by Edwards Brothers Malloy

CONTENTS

Acknowledgements	viii
How to use this book	x
Introductory notes	1
Riddles	3
Clues	32
Background information	43
Indices	148
Bibliography	155
Resources for further exploration	184

Some people write about the past. Some people live in it. Some manage to learn from it and use that knowledge to help build a better future; shaping history moment by moment, through their actions, in the present. This book is dedicated to two exceptional people who have consistently worked to build a better future, often under exceptionally difficult conditions.
To Lena Nemirovskaya and Yury Senokossov.
May history be kind to you.

Acknowledgements

There are many people to whom I owe a debt of thanks, for without their help and support, this book would not have been published. The majority of these will necessarily remain unsung. They form part of a huge number of people who have engaged positively with the Internet and made the best of it what it is – the collective effort of serious historians, curators, librarians, specialists, independent researchers, academics, web designers, archivists and programmers is overwhelming. My heartfelt thanks goes out to all of you.

I would like to extend particular thanks to my wife and daughter – your patience and willingness to test out so many of these riddles over mealtime discussions, when you would probably much rather have been discussing dogs, recipes and the latest film-related gossip is much appreciated. I would like to thank Mike Ellwood for permission to include one of his poems in the book; my colleague, Giles Abbott, for his generosity in sharing his expertise in storytelling; and David Pinto, for his inspiration and commitment to the whole concept of Odyssey Grids. My thanks also to Rodric Braithwaite and Alessandro Scafi for reading through the manuscript and making suggestions for improvements; to Alice Walters for her advice and to Teresa Monachino for her work on the cover design; and last but not least, my students, who continue to inspire me to become a better teacher and challenge me to keep finding new ways to make learning interesting for them.

I am particularly grateful to the team at John Hunt Publishing for their support.

I am grateful for all the corrections I have received and the result is as accurate as I have been able to get it. However, if it turns out I have made an error of fact or judgement, I have done so unknowingly – and as I believe it's better to know that I've made a mistake than not to know that I could have corrected one, I welcome any feedback which will allow me to knowingly correct mine.

How to use this book

This book contains 30 short stories written as riddles, or cultural 'whodunits' relating to major historical figures and events. Framed in this form, I've found the riddles can't help but engage people's imagination and broaden their horizons.

The collection is designed to be used as part of an Odyssey Grid journey – if you're not familiar with Odyssey Grids, you can find out about these innovative non-linear, content-free, scalable educational displays which have engagement and inspiration built into them in the book David Pinto and I wrote: *Odyssey: Dynamic Learning System*, Alresford: Liberalis Books, 2014.

These riddles can be used in educational establishments – as part of Odyssey journeys conducted in individual classrooms, for instance, or as an Odyssey journey set up as a whole-school, development-stage or year-group assembly activity at the start of the week, with the content dictating an approach for that week for each subject that is studied in the school. The links can be solid or tenuous, but they will help integrate understanding of the way subjects interrelate. Each riddle has a range of activity suggestions relating to most subjects covered by major national curricula (eg music, modern foreign languages, geography, science, mathematics, literature and the arts). You can access a sample and find out more details about this add-on feature on the Odyssey Grid website: www.odysseygrids.com. Each cultural riddle has an enigmatic title. This is what I would recommend putting up on an Odyssey grid piece. Feel free to make up your own titles that resonate best with you.

The riddles can also be enjoyed, outside the context of an Odyssey Grid, for their own sake. They can be used in schools; by facilitators on training courses; by parents with children, over meal times, during car journeys, or at bedtimes. In business, they can be used to enhance internal communications.

And they can, of course, be used by you, as an individual reader, just for fun. They're meant to be fun. That's one of the main reasons why I wrote them.

I hope you have at least as much fun engaging with them as I've had putting them together – if not more. I hope others around the globe will contribute their perspectives and stories to this series to enrich and expand the offering to the benefit of all those who experience them, whether as readers, or listeners.

But however you plan to approach the riddles, here's a little secret – and it's a secret that applies equally whether you're facilitating an Odyssey journey, or whether you're just engaging with the riddles on your own: the riddles work best when they get under a guesser's skin.

Don't worry about the feeling of being in a space of 'not knowing' for longer than is comfortable, or allowing others to experience the feeling when facilitating an Odyssey journey. This is when deeper, more lasting connections are made between existing knowledge and the knowledge hinted at in these riddles. Although it may not feel like fun at the time, you'll get a bigger buzz from solving it yourself – or letting others solve it for themselves – in the long run.

Enjoy!

Leon Conrad, London, UK
May 2014

Introductory notes

The one duty we owe to history is to rewrite it.
Oscar Wilde

These history riddles come from a wide range of cultures over a time span that stretches over nearly 4,500 years.

The content of the stories has given them a widespread appeal. They generally start as culturally specific and stretch out to have universal significance. They draw on scenes that go beyond their initial cultural settings of time and place to become part of the history and stories of the human race.

This common element of cultural resonance has been central to the selection process – these are stories that have either stood the test of time, or resonate on a universal level. The older ones are ones that have typically grown in the telling over time. Often there's something heroic about them.

Hoopoe is an example of a story selected for its strong cultural resonance to provoke discussion, exploration and research. Its protagonist appears in Jewish, Islamic, and Christian holy books, crossing over to the myths and legends of these cultures as well.

The protagonist of **Never Man** is very much a product of a particular time and place in history. His influence, however, extended far beyond the geographical boundaries of his country and writers all over the world have spun out stories about him with equal fascination.

Elephants is rooted in history, but the story takes on extra significance when mixed with Greek myth. **Blast!** tells a story of a man who resorts to desperate measures taken for the sake of deep-seated beliefs. It's a theme that's common to many more stories from different times and places, and discussions that explore this commonality will be particularly rewarding.

The stories are based on elements that appear, get changed, move around and get transformed through various tellings. Both this cross-fertilisation of elements and the universality of their underlying themes are why I think these stories have lasted. This collection is presented as part of this ongoing tradition – as a stepping stone in the (re)creation and addition to our shared global cultural heritage, with figures from more recent history included to bring the collection up to date. Some will appeal to the more imaginatively inclined, others to the more factually inclined. Hopefully they'll inspire an interest in history, a love of fiction and a respect for the long tradition of evoking the past to illuminate the present through the power of story.

The riddles in this collection are arranged by increasing word count just to keep you on your toes. Keys at the bottom of each story give page references to clues and to background notes for each of the cultural riddles, both of which are arranged in alphabetical order to make them easier for you to find. The background information ends with suggestions for further exploration and references to bibliographic sources which can be found in the bibliography at the end of the book. Indices of riddles arranged in alphabetical order by title, in chronological order, and in suggested thematic groupings are also included.

A note on sources

Classical sources, which are widely available in translation and original text, in print and on line, have been referenced giving author and title of work. Online editions where hyperlinked in the e-book editions of this work may, in a few cases, point to different editions simply because they are readily available on line.

All links to online resources given were live as at 1 May 2014. If a resource appears to be unavailable, some intelligent searching may be required to find it as websites are sometimes restructured. If this doesn't work, you can always search for it on the Internet Archive's *Wayback Machine* at www.archive.org.

Riddles

Bang!

Bang!
A list is nailed to a church door.
Bang!
The printing press spits out another copy of the list.
Bang!
The list lands in the hands of people in the marketplace and its contents hit their hearts.
Bang!
The list lands on the Pope's desk.
Bang!
We're still experiencing the effects today.

- What was so special about that bit of paper?
- Who's produced it and why?
- And what are the effects we're experiencing today?

[Clues: page 32; Background information: page 52]

Vision

A man emerges exhausted from dancing for twenty-four hours in a state of fasting and self-denial, his arms punctured with wounds. Standing with difficulty; proud, strong, drawing on superhuman strength, he makes a supreme effort to address the other members of his tribe and other tribal allies. They listen in awed silence as he speaks of dangerous times ahead, a vision of hostile warriors, reduced to the size of insects, falling head down from the sky into their territory. They look at each other, knowing they are in the presence of someone who is in touch with the Great Spirit.

- Who is this man?
- What does his vision describe?
- What happens as a result?

[Clues: page 41; Background information: page 140]

G

My face has been shaped with a metal file; my shoulder grooved; my foot nicked. My face has been covered in soot to see what I look like in mirror image. I've been thrust into red hot flames to harden me; plunged into a bucket of water to temper me. I've sired many offspring that form groups and families to make powerful marks wherever people use them. I'm small, but powerful. So powerful I've changed the world.

I started off in the Far East, but revolutionised European history when I was recreated by a German goldsmith, entrepreneur and inventor in Mainz.

- What am I?
- Who was this German goldsmith who recreated me?
- And what are we most famous for?

[Clues: page 35; Background information: page 81]

Pine Tree

Rome, 104 CE. The superintendent for the banks of the Tiber, an intelligent man, in his early 40s; a man who's well-known as a writer and thinker, is finally writing a letter – something he's been putting off for a while, because of the memories it brings back, memories of his uncle's tragic death 25 years previously, of a column of smoke like a pine tree, around 20 miles high, of unbearable heat, of a grey cloud that settled over a huge area, how he watched from a distance, powerless to help, unable to resist the huge force of nature. He's been asked to write about his uncle's death by a colleague, who is a historian and wants to write a true account of what happened.

- Who is the writer?
- Who was his uncle?
- And what caused his uncle's death?

[Clues: page 37; Background information: page 98]

Sealed

We're in an open field alongside the River Thames in Surrey, not far from Windsor Castle. We're here to stand up and say enough is enough. We've had enough of excessive taxation. We've had enough of oppression. We've had enough of injustice. We're here to stand up for justice. We're here to stand up for ideas which are more powerful than men. We're here to stand up for the freedom of our church and our country. We crowd round a tall man in purple robes as he reads from a document. He's addressing the king – a lean, seated figure, who is increasingly unhappy about what he's hearing. If he wants us to follow him, he will have to put his seal on this document. Blackmail? Perhaps. But enough is enough.

- Where are we?
- Why?
- And what will the king do?

[Clues: page 38; Background information: page 105]

Asp

We're in a monumentally large, forbidding building, built like a palace. Huge rooms are supported by columns. The central colonnade which cuts through them is lit with oil lamps. The walls beyond are painted with life-sized figures in vivid colours

– figures of strange animal-headed people in various poses. At the end of the colonnade, in the largest and furthest room, a group of women gather – they look sad, nervous, afraid. They are grouped around the central figure. This figure, a woman, is lying on a raised, bed-like structure decorated with pictograms of birds, feathers, lions, baskets, cartouches and other graphic symbols. Her face is incredibly beautiful. Her skin is clear and her complexion unblemished and yet she looks pale – deathly pale. She reaches her hand out towards a basket of figs beside her. She doesn't choose one, but extends her hand deeper into the basket, waiting for something to happen ...

- Who is she?
- What is she waiting for?
- And why?

[Clues: page 32; Background information: page 49]

Revolution

Paris, 1793. A young woman is holding an older woman's head in her hands. The young woman trembles slightly – she's afraid. She's been asked to make a model of the older woman's face by the people who are now in power. Her life, literally, depends on it. As she shapes the plaster cast, she remembers how not long ago this woman ruled over millions; she'd had the prettiest farm in the country where she loved to play with her friends, looking after the animals and making them look beautiful. When she was younger, she'd played games with Mozart. Now … she's gone. Her world no longer exists, and the young woman is left holding her severed head. As she waits for the plaster to harden on the death mask, she wonders what will happen when she finishes. Will it please the people who have asked her to make it? If she succeeds, they say she will live. If she fails, will they send her back to prison? Will they chop off her head? Will they kill her anyway?

- Who is the young woman?
- Whose head is she holding in her lap?
- And what do you think she might be best known for today?

[Clues: page 37; Background information: page 103]

A Photo Shoot?!

A young man and a young woman are sitting at a kitchen table in a house in the countryside. They're brother and sister. Visibly nervous and shocked, he's telling her the story of something that happened the day before in the big house on the nearby estate, where he had recently been appointed as a guard: of how at 2 o'clock that morning, the family, who were living under house arrest there, had been ordered to gather in a basement room to have a family photograph taken. The head of the family stood in the centre of the room; his 13-year-old son, only half-awake, sat on a chair to his right. Behind him, against the wall, stood his wife and their four daughters. A few of the household staff had been assembled as well. "And then …" the young boy faltered, reaching out to touch his sister's arm, continuing in a low voice, "… they killed them. They killed them all!"

- Who was killed?
- By whom?
- Why?
- Where did it happen?
- And what do you think the sister's reaction was?

[Clues: page 32; Background information: page 45]

Time!

We're on a flat stretch of ground, looking out to sea on a crisp, late summer day watching a group of men playing bowls. We're dressed – as they are – in doublets and hose, with white ruffs and velvet hats trimmed with feathers and thin, sharp swords at our belts.

Suddenly, we catch sight of a line of beacons being swiftly lit along the coast. As the line reaches the nearest beacon, a messenger rushes up, bows and urges us to go down to the coast to board the fleet of ships that's waiting down there. We're under attack.

We watch and wait as the players turn to the most senior person in their party – some excitedly, some nervously – and await his orders. The tension in us mounts like the flames in the beacons.

"Gentlemen, I suggest we finish our game before going out and punishing these upstarts for interrupting our fun."

We watch as they finish their game, then follow them down to the coast…

What happens next?

[Clues: page 40; Background information: page 131]

Shells

"Hey! Look out to sea! There's the emperor's trireme – that big ship with the three banks of oars. The trumpeters are getting ready to play a fanfare. Listen. He's probably going to give a speech in a minute. It's nearly a hundred years since Caesar landed in Britain and we have a situation. There's fighting in Britain and we're being sent to sort it out. There aren't that many of us and it's been a long, hard march through Germania down to the coast of Gaul. And now, here we are, on the coast of Gaul, being ordered to get the battle gear ready. So, on the north stretch of the beach, some of the legionaries are checking the stone-throwing machines we call *ballistae*; to the south, others are setting up the large dart-throwing machines we call *catapultae* ... but wait. What's that he's saying? He wants us to gather a whole lot of seashells? And why's he dressed like that? Who does he think he is? Venus?"

- Who is this emperor?
- Why have the soldiers been asked to gather seashells?
- And why is he dressed this way?

[Clues: page 38; Background information: page 112]

KKM

We're at a huge building site at the edge of a hot sandy desert on the western shore of one of the longest rivers in the world. In front of us are three structures. These structures are so huge they take your breath away. The last is still under construction. The sloping walls of the structures gleam brightly in the heat of the sun. We've come to pay our respects, for this is a burial site of three great rulers. While the last is still alive, this is where he will be buried when he dies. The sound of stonecutters' chisels ring out off the rocks, along with the chants of workers pulling heavy blocks in place, interspersed with creaking of machinery and the shouts of overseers – sounds that have been echoing around this site for decades. We sit and watch and as dusk falls and the sounds quieten, the stars in the night sky shine brightly down with Orion, the brightest of them all, the Dog Star, clearly visible.

- Where are we?
- When?
- What are the structures?
- And for whom were they built?

[Clues: page 36; Background information: page 87]

Blast!

On a dark November night, a tall, thin man wearing a tall black hat and a sweeping black cloak crept between the narrow streets of the town lined with wooden houses, carrying a lantern. He was heading towards an empty storehouse near a palace which backed on to a river. He entered the building nervously, looking over his shoulder to make sure that no one had followed him. He hesitated, checking to see if anyone was hiding out inside, closing the door behind him only once he was sure he was alone. Inside, in the light of the lantern, he checked the piles of firewood that he and his friends had placed at the end of the room, under which they'd hidden some barrels. Finding them as he'd left them, he put the lantern down carefully and settled down to wait. He thought about the plan he and his friends had hatched up. Tomorrow was the big day. The palace would be full. And when it was, that's when he'd do the deed. Until then, all he had to do was sit, wait, and guard the barrels.

- Who was the man?
- Where was he?
- And what was he planning to do?

[Clues: page 33; Background information: page 61]

Never Man

It's a summer's day in dark times. A fierce war is being waged across four continents with over thirty countries drawn into the conflict. And a 65-year-old man, a high-ranking official from a noble family who's spent his life in political service to his country, steps out of a bunker near the western edge of the westernmost borough of London. Thoughtful, silent, he stands for a moment, turns and looks up at the air raid siren on the roof and the blue sky overhead. Beside him, his chief staff officer, thirteen years his junior, moves to say something, but the older man says, "Don't speak to me. I have never been so moved." He pauses, then walks purposefully yet thoughtfully towards the car parked by the entrance, waiting to take him back to London. After a while, the older man says something – a single sentence; powerful in form, deep in meaning – which strikes both of them.

That line was later heard by millions of people across the world. It helped boost a whole nation's morale, galvanise patriotic spirit and is still remembered today.

- Who were these two people?
- What was the occasion?
- And what was it the older man said that had such a strong impact?

[Clues: page 37; Background information: page 95]

Stars

We're heading North down Arch Street (in Philadelphia, Pennsylvania) towards the upholsterer's shop at number 89. We're looking for a pretty little narrow 2-story brick building with a pattern of black and red brickwork on the façade made of alternating glazed and unglazed bricks. We know we're there when we get to the small window with a sign with the owner's name, and fancy pillows, hand-embroidered waistcoats, table-cloths and other household furnishings on display. We enter to find the owner, a calm, gentle widow of medium height, with a core of steel, talking to a couple of clients.

The two men by her are wearing wigs, long frock coats with gold trimming, black shoes with bright brass buckles and white stockings. Each of the men holds his three-cornered hat in one hand. One of them is showing her a rough sketch of a design they've come to ask her to make up.

Pattern-cutting scissors in hand, she's snipping away at a piece of folded paper which she unfolds to reveal a regular shape. "Here. This is how I'd do it. Not difficult at all," she says.

- Who is she?
- Who are the men?
- And what have they come to ask her to make for them?

[Clues: page 39; Background information: page 123]

Maps

We're in the throne room of a Moorish palace. The room's high walls are richly decorated from top to bottom with bands of colourful interlacing lines and repeated geometric patterns. It's a warm day and the calming sounds of birds chirping and water cascading gently from a fountain at the centre of a long rectangular pool outside permeate the room. Servants usher a man in. He enters, carrying a bundle of maps and artefacts. He's tall; in his forties; his eyes are lively; he's wearing a smart, long, plain brown tunic; a short brown cloak; and a black and silver cross hanging from a silver chain around his neck. He kneels at the feet of a royal couple in an attitude of humble nobility. When told to rise, he does so slowly, with dignity. They start to talk. During the conversation, he rolls out a map and points westwards to where the wide, empty ocean sea is shown. The king and queen listen. She seems more interested in the cross he's wearing than in what he's saying. It's taken him 6 years of negotiation to get to this point – scholars have looked over his plans before and shaken their heads.

- Who is the man with the maps?
- Who is the man he's talking to?
- What do they think of his plan?
- And why does the queen seem more interested in the cross the man wears around his neck than the ideas he's been talking to them about?

[Clues: page 36; Background information: page 94]

Bones

We're in a long, painted medieval hall. The walls are decorated with angels which have been painted with peacock feathers and saints painted with squirrels' tails; the ceiling with stars, painted with down from the breasts of royal swans. There's a meeting taking place. It's a meeting of a group of men that are chosen to be part of it when the need arises. The group's members have been meeting in this room since 1547. A figure in a long gown stands up to speak, but the leader of the group interrupts him. He's impatient. He points to one of the group's members. "You're just a juggler." He points to two others. "You're whoremasters." "You're a drunkard," he shouts at another. "And you're cheating the public. I won't stand for it." He beckons to one of the soldiers standing at the door and gives him an order. "Take away that fool's bauble," he says, pointing to a long ornamental stick made of gold. He declares the group was no longer fit to carry the name it has been given and turns everyone out of the house, shouting, "Depart, I say. In the name of God, go!" and locks the doors behind them.

- Who was the man?
- What was the group he had just disbanded?
- And why?

[Clues: page 33; Background information: page 65]

Terrible Twos

Some say it never happened.
Some say it only happened to a few people.
Some say it happened to thousands.

Others ... well, they stay silent. The grief is too great to allow them to speak.

For those that hear it, the noise is deafening. The kind of noise that makes your brain spin, your guts turn, your eyes water, your body reel. You're unlikely to hear the like of it, and you'll be thankful for that. Thankful you'll never hear what they hear: the cries of mothers in mourning; the cries of dying children, run through by spears; the thud and splat of babies' heads bashed against rocks; the cries of fathers dying while trying to save their youngest sons – not one of them over two years old. Some older children are speechless. Some are adding their howls to the general cacophony. [One child, probably the same age as you, is curled up in a corner, hugging a dog, finding comfort in the warm fur and the wet tongue licking the boy's face clean where the blood of his baby brother has spurted over it.] This was such a nice place before the King ordered the slaughter. Why would he do such a thing? Why here? Why now?

- Where is this scene set and when?
- Who was the king?
- And why had he given the order for all male children under the age of two to be killed?

Note

In a group setting, you may wish to omit the sentence in square brackets if you have sensitive people in your group.

[Clues: page 39; Background information: page 127]

Hoopoe

She was rich. She was beautiful. She was powerful. She was wise. And she started to hear stories – stories of a king who was rich, powerful, and handsome on top of it, and – so they said – was *also* wise. The wisest man in the world, they said. This was long, long before television or radio existed. Some say accounts of this king reached her through travellers, merchants, ambassadors and spies. Some say they were carried to her on the wings of a hoopoe. Travellers' tales? Writers' fantasies? Was he really rich, powerful, handsome, wise? Were these stories true? Were they lies? In her wisdom, she decided to set out to see for herself. Across the desert she travelled, in a grand procession carrying rich gifts of gold and spices, having sent ahead of her a fleet of ships carrying exotic woods, pearls, precious stones. Some say her journey took seven years. Seven years during which she met people who were wise, but would the man she met at the end of the journey be the wisest? On the journey she thought up questions to test him on. Here are four:

1. What is evil?
2. Are the eyes or the ears superior?
3. What is the most powerful organ of the body?
4. How are body and spirit connected?

- Who were these two people – the wisest of the wise?
- When did this happen?
- And what would your answers to these questions be?

[Clues: page 35; Background information: page 83]

Bees

We've had to leave home at 6 o'clock in the morning.

We've ridden through Paris on a cold winter afternoon to join around 20,000 people packed into a building in keen anticipation. It's chilly, despite the crowds. Friends wave, people chatter. The excitement mounts.

It's now around 11 o'clock. Outside, the sound of horses neighing, marching bands, gun salutes puncture the air.

The man we've come to see – the head of the nation he's led into war and out of war successfully; the man who's led the nation away from monarchy towards a republic – has arrived.

He's clothed in white tunic, pantaloons and stockings, with a richly decorated, heavy purple velvet cloak trimmed with ermine and decorated with golden bees.

The ceremony unfolds – with music sung by a choir of hundreds, prayers and readings.

At the high point of the ceremony, at the furthest end of the building which faces due east, he stands, lifts a golden crown specially made for the occasion and places it on his head. He turns, lifts another crown then turns back to walk down the short flight of steps to crown his wife, who kneels before him there.

He is the first person to be the centre of this particular rite in 1,000 years.

They both rise and process to the west end of the building where a specially erected arch, on a raised platform, stands at the top of a long flight of steps, overlooked on either side by spectators ranked in three tiers.

From there, the man stands in front of a gilded throne, upholstered in blue velvet, richly decorated in raised and padded goldwork embroidery and proclaims the oath which has been specially composed for the occasion.

- Who's the man in the story?
- What's the occasion?
- And when did this scene actually take place?

[Clues: page 33; Background information: page 57]

Stop!

We're in a long enclosed space with walls made of reed mats tied to wooden canes curved over our heads to form an arched ceiling. The outer edge of the space is framed by a group of men, women and children – members of the tribe whose land we're in. It's dark outside. There's a crescent moon hanging in a sky glittering with stars above. Within the building, a fire is sending up bright red sparks towards the ceiling as if straining to reach beyond it to the stars outside. At the far end of the building, on a raised platform, sits a powerful chief, in ritual costume, made of racoon skins, on a throne which looks like a bedstead.

A man is led towards him. He's dressed in black boots,

breeches, a linen shirt and doublet. His eyes have a steely look to them. He's strong, proud and wary. He has no reason to be afraid, but something tells him he should be ready to face death if he has to. The senior members of the tribe exchange words. The tribe members start to chant a ritual song, stamping, the men banging their spears as two large sacrificial stones are brought in and laid at the chief's feet. The man is forced to kneel in front of the chief and lay his head on one of the stones. The sounds of the women's voices piercing the night as they sing louder and louder. The chief stands over the victim. He pulls out a knife, raises his hand.

A voice from the crowd screams out, "Stop!" – a figure emerges from the throng and comes between him and the victim. The chief pauses.

The rest of the tribe fall silent.

- Who is the victim?
- Who is his saviour?
- Where is the victim from?
- And what happens next?

[Clues: page 39; Background information: page 126]

Stand Up!

A black-haired, smartly-dressed seamstress in her early forties, wearing glasses, is waiting at a bus stop. She's finished at the department store downtown and is heading home. It's just over ten years since the war ended. Life's good, but it's also tough – tough on some people in particular. But it's the 1st of December. The Christmas lights are up. Admiring them, she finds it isn't long before the bus arrives. The doors open. She gets on and pays her fare. She recognises the driver – not the friendliest one on the route, but she's on the bus now. She walks a short way down the aisle, with its grooved floor formed of narrow strips of hardwood, finds an empty seat on one of the rows of metal-framed seats covered with hard, green leather-effect plastic, and sits down. All she's focused on is just getting home. The bus stops and more people get on. Two stops later, the bus fills up. There's one person left standing at the front, and the bus driver turns and tells the four people in the row where the woman is sitting to stand up and make room for the last passenger who's got on. At first, nobody moves. He repeats his request, saying, "Y'all, make it light on yourselves and let me have those seats." Three people stand and do as he asks. This woman doesn't. The driver asks her whether she's going to move. "No, I'm not," she replies. It just doesn't seem fair. Why should they all have to move to free four seats, when there was only one needed? They'd paid the same fare, after all. "I'll have to call a policeman," said the driver. All the woman said was, "You may do that."

- Who was she?
- Why were the people in her row expected to give up their seats?
- Why do you think she refused?
- And what do you think happened next?

[Clues: page 38; Background information: page 116]

Bonfire

We're in a crowded market square in Rouen. We've come to see an execution. People around us in the crowd talk to each other in English. A cry goes up and we crane to catch a view of the 19-year-old girl who's being led to the stake where she will be burned alive. An English woman in the crowd, a merchant's wife, munching gingerbread, turns to her neighbour in the crowd and says:

"There she is, the 19-year-old witch. Mad as they come, they say. Thinks she's above us, she does. Says she sees saints and they bow down to her. Can you imagine? And she does things no woman should ever do – imagine wanting to dress like a man. I mean, it's not natural. It's against the law. It says so in the Bible, doesn't it? Look – they're lighting the pile of wood. She's going to get her just deserts, she is. And we're here to see it. This is going to be something to tell our grandchildren about, for sure."

And on the other side of the square, a priest from the neighbouring parish turns to the local baker, saying:

"I can't believe they're doing this to this poor, innocent girl, this child of God. An enemy of the church? No way. I'm convinced she's an instrument of God – if God created the universe and everything in it, why shouldn't He have made her His instrument? Look how she's holding the wooden cross that was put together for her when she asked for one, just now. There's real beauty in her faith. It's pitiful to think that she's only here because her own people betrayed her. Shame on us. Shame! May her death come quickly and may God have mercy on our souls."

- Who was the girl?
- Who had ordered her execution?
- What crime had she committed?
- What influence did she have both during her life and after her death?

[Clues: page 34; Background information: page 70]

Life and Death

We're in a hot courtroom, where a man accused of treason, of plotting a revolution that would overthrow the government, is about to stand up to speak. This near the Tropic of Capricorn, even though it's an April afternoon, the temperature in the white-walled room, with its high ceiling and arched stained glass windows seems as hot as a blast furnace.

Despite this, the man speaks for over two hours.

He's on trial because he'd chosen to fight; to lay down his life, if need be; to fight for people's right to a decent life. Now … he's fighting … for his life.

He's part of a majority that's ruled by a minority that has no share in how their country's governed. The members of this majority aren't allowed to work anywhere but the town in which they were born. They aren't allowed to buy homes, only to rent them. They aren't allowed to live anywhere but in ghettoes. They aren't allowed to be out after 11 o'clock at night. They aren't allowed to travel in their own country to seek work.

What he's fighting for, above all, are equal political rights, harmony and freedom for all. These are the ideals he's spent most of his life fighting for.

He turns to the judge, the man who has the power to condemn him to death, or let him live, and declares – to his face – that these are ideals for which he is, if necessary, prepared to die.

He sits down and the court is adjourned while the judge considers his verdict. The trial drags on. Months pass and the day comes when the judge is set to deliver his sentence. Outside the courtroom, crowds of people have gathered, waiting for the verdict to be read out.

When it is, it sends shockwaves round the world, provokes debates in the United Nations, protest vigils and ongoing marches and campaigns.

- Who was this man?
- What was his sentence?
- What was his role in his country's political life?

[Clues: page 36; Background information: page 89]

15

Rome. 15 March, in the 709th year after the founding of Rome.

Last night's thunderstorm has cleared. It's a bright day, but there's a dark mood hanging over the city.

The general's been told not to go to the senate today.

His wife's told him not to 'cause she had a bad dream.

The priests of Rome have told him not to 'cause they've read bad news in the entrails of the animals they've sacrificed this morning.

His mistress is concerned.

But the general's obstinate. He calls for his purple tunic, wraps it round his white toga, puts on his laurel crown, the sign of victory the senate has honoured him with and he leaves for the senate. After all, he's more than just a general. He's been elected a consul and a dictator – although some would say he's weak because he has a history of stammering, he's a powerful statesman. And yet, he's most comfortable thinking of himself as a general, because today, being a general means something. Armies don't fight for the senate any more. They fight for generals. And the senate hates that. But the people love him for it. And well they might, for this is no ordinary general.

He's written books and built Rome's first public library; he's built new roads and set up a police force to protect travellers on them; he's made canals and set up new irrigation systems, and set up a new calendar.

He's carried in his litter down the long road that's called the Via Sacra or the Sacred Way that leads to the Theatre of Pompey. The crowds cheer when they see him.

As he gets out of his litter, he sees his best friend who tries to approach him to warn him not to go into the senate, but someone holds his friend back and the general goes on to climb the white marble stairs that lead to the room in which the senate is meeting today.

What happens next?

[Clues: page 32; Background information: page 43]

Revolt

"Well here's a change. Rather different from making sure a road gets built straight and that it ultimately leads to Rome! And a nice change from governing a city – mind you, it's a while since I've been on a battlefield. I'd better get some practice in before I leave for Gaul." And so he did. And by the time he reached the coast with his troops, he felt ready for anything. The one thing he wasn't expecting was for the soldiers to revolt. "It's the end of the world!" they said. "We're not going beyond it!" He tried to reason with them. "You think the coast of Gaul is the end of the known world? The coast of Gaul is not, by any means, the end of the known world. Not by far. We've been trading with the people over the sea since Julius Caesar went over some 80 years ago. I've read his book on the country. We know what it's like. Lots of rain and bogs, I'm told, but good pickings for us if we're successful." But his speech had the same effect as reciting Shakespeare to a stubborn donkey that was refusing to get into a boat. Whatever he said had no effect. He was just about to give up and go back, but he didn't. You know what got them into those boats in the end? One of the emperor's friends dressing up and putting on a show for them. The soldiers laughed so much, they declared it to be the best Saturnalia show they'd ever seen – and decided they were in for a good laugh, so set off with their ballistas, their catapults and elephants, got in their boats, and sailed across the water, ready to fight to the death. Halfway across, the weather turned against them and they would have turned back too had they not seen a flash of lightning light up the white cliffs ahead and show them how near they were to land.

- Where were these soldiers heading?
- And how did the battle go?

[Clues: page 37; Background information: page 101]

Elephants

We're in the middle of an army camp, high up in the Alps. Behind us, the mountains slope down towards Gaul. Ahead of us, the mountains slope down towards Italy. On either side, the mountain range stretches out, like a huge curved bow. The camp we're in is near the top of a mountain range, on a plateau about 2,188 metres above sea level. Our journey started on the Iberian coast, but our departure was delayed. It's November and it's getting colder. Many men and beasts have died in the crossing so far. The conditions are getting harsher and there are small bands of fighters living in the mountains that don't want us to pass. We face a snowstorm and a steep, slippery descent ahead, with the ever-present threat of avalanches and landslides. The fighters launch surprise attacks on us whenever they can. We've gathered whatever food we could find on our way, but it's not much.

We're being led on by a young, rugged, dark-olive-skinned man, who's a strong fighter. While only 29, he commands the respect of his entire army. He's led us through countryside surrounded by snow, glaciers, through rocky terrain and fought off many of the attacks from the hostile mountain-dwellers.

We've followed him because he's inspired us. He said, "Whatever a single man can do, an army can do. And an army can do it because it is only a large number of soldiers; soldiers who are much more than single men; soldiers who carry with them much more than the weapons of war; soldiers who can meet any difficulty with the courage and energy that makes them more than men. You are such soldiers. You've crossed the Pyrenees. You can cross the Alps." And so here we are. We've been travelling for nine days so far, along a path across the Alps that only the legendary Hercules has ever been known to travel up to now. We're about to rest for a couple of days, and we'll be joined by some of our companions who fell down mountain slopes, were injured in fighting, and by horses that have managed to climb out of crevices and limp after us, following our tracks.

- When in history is this happening?
- Where is the army headed and why?
- And who is their leader?

[Clues: page 35; Background information: page 78]

Travellers' Tales

We've been invited to dinner at the house of a family of rich merchants (known as a palace in the local dialect) to celebrate their return from their travels in the East. We've travelled there through a series of winding waterways on a boat manned by a single oarsman. The meal's been fantastic – rich food, exquisitely prepared with rare, exotic spices.

The merchants have been away for 24 years. Everyone thought they'd died abroad, and when they returned from their travels, they were dressed so shabbily and sounded so foreign, the rest of the family apparently refused to let them into the house for ages.

At the end of the meal, the table's cleared. A pile of rags is brought in and put at the head of the table, in front of the youngest of the three merchants. He stands up and starts to speak. The older two – his father and uncle – lean back and listen. Despite his foreign way of speaking, he's a born storyteller. He tells us stories of their travels, of the strange sights and customs he, his father, and his uncle have seen: of princes, princesses, emperors and khans. As he speaks he takes us with him to lands we've only heard of as legends … to China, to Xanadu, to the farthest reaches of Asia and back; of Bokhara, Mongolia, Armenia, Trebizond, and of the great emperor Kublai Khan, who is served by magicians who make cups travel through the air to him when he wants to drink.

As he speaks, the young man reaches out to a pile of rags on the table in front of him, those shabby clothes the three men wore when they arrived – clothes which aren't at all what you'd expect members of a family of wealthy merchants to wear – and starts to cut them up.

As he does so, the shabby pile of rags in front of him reveal glints of light reflected off the many jewels hidden in the seams and in the lining. Soon the walls appear as colourful as the gleaming glass mosaics in the interior of the magnificent cathedral in the town's main square by the lagoon.

Everyone around the table receives a handsome jewel as a gift, but the greatest of all these gifts are the stories he's brought back. Everyone agrees he must write them down. Maybe he will one day. If he does end up writing a book, I'll definitely pay someone to copy it out for me.

- Where are we?
- Who are these merchants?
- Where have they been?
- What's so special about them?
- If these stories are ever written down, why would you need to pay someone to copy them out?
- And what's the cathedral referred to in the riddle?

[Clues: page 40; Background information: page 133]

Cinders

We're in a remote cottage in Somerset, where a young but grey-haired pagan Saxon farmer's wife with a lined face, calloused hands and sinewy body, hands on hips, is looking at the troubled man sitting by her fire, mending his bow. He'd knocked on the door a twilight ago and asked her if she could put him up for the night so he could mend his weapons before he went back into the forest to continue fighting the Danes, who were gaining the upper hand in the struggle for dominance of the country.

She was a cautious, but loyal Saxon. She'd showed him in, but had told him she wasn't going to stand for any trouble. He was tall and broad-shouldered, but she had a pitchfork behind the door and a knife at her belt. He'd sworn he meant her no harm and for some reason she trusted him. His face was dirty, his uniform worn, and his woollen cloak fastened with an elaborate clasp. He was obviously a soldier and he reminded her of her husband, who was fighting alongside the Saxons. The man was well-spoken enough, although he was a bit dirty. You get that in wartime. She hoped someone would do the same for her husband if he needed help, irrespective of whether they were Christian or pagan. But her husband wasn't here and she had to do everything around the house, so she decided to put her guest to work.

"Don't just sit there mending your bow expecting to do nothing round the house. You can watch these loaves while I go and bring in the sheep and feed the chickens. Make sure the loaves don't burn, now." And she bustled off. The man smiled sadly to himself as he fletched another arrow, wondering if they'd ever succeed in clearing the Danes from the country, then lost himself in thought again as he settled down to fletch some new arrows, singing quietly to himself.

Half an hour later, the farmer's wife came back and found him singing quietly to himself, completely ignoring the fact that the loaves that had been baking over the fire had started to burn.

"Can't you even mind the loaves, man? Can't you smell the burning? Slow to stop the food burning, yet you'd want to be first to eat it, probably – if we ever get round to eating, with you in charge, that is. Your singing isn't that bad, though. You could do something with that voice. Just stay away from cooking. Cooking up trouble's all you're probably good for. Get up and help me lay the table, man. I never saw anything like it. It's a good thing you're not running the country!"

- Who was the man?
- Why was he so preoccupied?
- And what did he end up doing with his singing?

[Clues: page 34; Background information: page 74]

Webs

A man sits in a room in his house lined with wood panels, with 2,000 books lining the walls around him. I say house, it's really more like a castle – a castle dating from the 1600s – which this writer, storyteller and lover of history has called 'a plaything in stone'. He's had it built this way, in the border lands between Scotland and England, near the River Tweed, both to fulfil his own fantasy vision and to create a home for his family worthy of his new status as a Baronet.

You'd think he was happy, but you'd be wrong. He's feeling miserable, for two reasons: (1) the house is no longer his. Two years ago, he was rich, but now, after a big financial crash which was no fault of his, his house belongs to his creditors, who have allowed him to continue to live there with his family to continue writing to pay back what he owes. And (2) his grandson is sick. On a recent visit, remembering how awful he found it to be sick as a child and how having polio had left him with a permanent limp, he'd been telling him stories about the history of Scotland. Having just returned from a trip to London, he's decided to write the stories down and, at the same time, hopefully produce a work that will sell well and that might help clear off a bit of his debt. "My own right hand shall do it," he declares. He picks up his pen and starts to spin a new story – a story about a Scottish King, who had good reason to feel miserable. It's 1307. He's been wracked with guilt at having killed his rival, John Comyn, in front of the altar of the Church of the Minorites in Dumfries the previous year. He's just heard that his sister has been put in a cage by the English King who's been marching on Scotland and gaining territory there. What's more, this English King has ordered that the heads of two of the Scottish King's brothers be cut off and has banished the Scottish King's daughter to an English convent. He's just about ready to give up. "I'd be better off just forgetting about Scotland," he thinks. "I should renounce the throne, dismiss my followers and go on a crusade to the Holy Land to recapture Jerusalem and ask for forgiveness for my sins there. On the other hand, what good would it do my wife? If I'm going to fight, wouldn't I be putting my energy to better use in trying to fight the English and restore Scotland to the Scots?" Caught up in his thoughts, he looks up at the ceiling and sees a spider trying to set up a web between two wooden beams. Six times has the king fought against the English. Six times has the spider started to spin a thread, attached it, travelled back across it, only to have the thread break. The king watches, fascinated as the spider tries for a seventh time – spins a thread, attaches it, travels back across it ... will it make it? Either way, should the king take it as an omen? Should he keep on trying, or should he give up?

- What do you think?
- What do you think the spider did?
- How does this affect the king?
- And who's the man writing the story?

[Clues: page 41; Background information: page 143]

Torches

A philosopher meets a boy when the boy is 12 and he's 15. The philosopher becomes the boy's tutor.

Now, 19 years later, the boy's an emperor and he's just ordered the philosopher to take his own life.

"I should have seen it coming. The boy's mother, who was then the empress, was always ambitious for her son. I could see it plainly when she appointed me as his tutor 19 years ago. When she married the emperor, who was also her uncle, she made sure he adopted her boy as his own, and greased her son's path to the throne with blood. The first years weren't so bad. The young emperor, who was then 17, accepted my advice and the boy's excesses were limited to doing things like singing and performing in public, or having gold and silk nets made so that he could use them when he went fishing. Then things got worse. He was worried that his mother hated his new girlfriend and had concerns about how he was ruling. He was terrified she'd try to have him poisoned, so he tried to kill her more than once. He botched it up several times, but eventually succeeded. He built increasingly lavish palaces; and greedy for land, got his henchmen to set fire to the best buildings in Rome. He watched from a high tower, as temples, bronze statues from Greece, books, libraries were turned to slag and ash, while he dressed up in costume and sang an epic about Troy going up in flames, accompanying himself on the lyre. He blamed the arson on the Christians and wreaked such punishment on them I shudder to think of it. I guess I should be grateful he's ordered me to commit suicide and hasn't had me covered in the flayed skins of an animal to be torn to pieces by hunting dogs, or crucified, or smeared with pitch and used as a living torch to light one of his garden parties – parties he's partly financed with the wealth I've freely given him to try to protect myself and preserve my own life. I've given him my riches, my country villas and gardens, my palace in Rome. They said I had 500 exquisite tables of citrus wood with ivory feet – all identical – who could have that many? Is that what they'll remember of me after I die? How many tables I had? Will they remember any of my books – my philosophical works, my scientific ones? Will anyone perform my plays, or my satire? Perhaps one day the memory of my suffering will bring someone delight. How many new animals have I come to know for the first time in my lifetime? How many will be discovered after I die? It would be nice to be able to live to see them, but it's not going to be. I had nothing to do with the plot to assassinate the emperor, but will they believe that? Should I accept death as a welcome release from the weight of worry this emperor's reign has brought or fight to stay alive to prove my innocence, to enjoy what time remains for me of the years the fates have ordained? Even if I wanted to, would I be allowed to?"

The philosopher reaches for a writing instrument, but the tribune who's just delivered the emperor's decree shakes his head and tells him not to bother writing a will. All his property has been confiscated by the state. Left with no possessions, the philosopher turns to his wife and two of their friends who they'd been visiting and wills them the legacy of his life: his way of living; his way of dying. When his wife offers to commit suicide with him, he accepts the gift and orders the slaves to run a warm bath. He writes a few words to bring his last book to a close, puts down his writing instrument and prepares himself for death.

His last words to his friends have been immortalised in verse by the poet Mike Ellwood:

Virtuous friends, death now or hereafter
Is immaterial. We live, we die.
We may laugh in poverty; in wealth, cry.
The wind erases all our tears or laughter.
Death crushes him only who, despite fame,
Does not know himself, nor accepts his faults
Or the worthlessness of that on which he dotes.
But he who is humble dies without blame.

Beware the mindless wilderness that lurks
Forever in the darkness of men's greed.
But see, above, how heaven's countless sparks
Illuminate the night like scattered seed.
See, slowly rising, as my blood is drawn,
The sun of understanding in the crimson dawn.

- Who is the emperor?
- Who is the philosopher?

- And how has each of them influenced the development of our civilisation?

[Clues: page 40; Background information: page 132]

Clues

page 20 ☚ 15 ☛ page 43

1. His mistress was a very famous queen.
2. Shakespeare wrote a play about the general.
3. This took place in 44 BCE.
4. The main character in the scene is famous for saying *veni, vidi, vici* (I came, I saw, I conquered).
5. He's also famous for saying *alea jacta est* (the die is cast).

page 7 ☚ A Photo Shoot?! ☛ page 45

1. The event sent emotional shock waves across the world at the time.
2. There is an imperial connection here.
3. The event took place in Russia.
4. The event took place in 1918.
5. One of the women who was shot was called Anastasia.

page 5 ☚ Asp ☛ page 49

1. The woman, in her time, was considered one of the most beautiful women in the world.
2. She has inspired many works of literature.
3. The woman is a famous queen.
4. She went to meet her first lover rolled up in a carpet.
5. The scene reputedly took place in Alexandria.

page 3 ☚ Bang! ☛ page 52

1. The scene takes place in a town called Wittenberg.
2. The list has 95 items on it.
3. The Pope was Giovanni di Lorenzo de' Medici, who took the name of Pope Leo X.
4. The man who nailed them to the church door was both a monk (Augustinian) and a priest (Catholic).

5. A famous twentieth century civil rights activist called Michael [King] changed his name to Martin [L. King] in honour of the man who came up with this list.

page 15 ☜ Bees ☞ page 57

1. The building is Notre Dame Cathedral.
2. This ceremony took place a few months before Napoleon was crowned King of Italy.
3. The event happened on a day called *Cire,* the day of wax, the 11th of *Frimaire,* the 3rd month of the 13th year in the Republican Calendar, one of the coldest months of the year.
4. The man is a leader of men and a lover of women.
5. The man is traditionally thought of as short. He was 5.5 feet (1.68 metres) tall.

page 9 ☜ Blast! ☞ page 61

1. The event took place in London.
2. It took place when James I and VI was on the throne.
3. The fact that the event took place in November is significant.
4. It took place early in November.
5. People generally believe the man was hiding out underground rather than on ground level.

page 12 ☜ Bones ☞ page 65

1. The man's surname has 7 letters in it, but you probably won't find this helpful.
2. The man who stood up to speak initially but was interrupted was a Speaker.
3. The group's name has something to do with the French word for speaking.
4. The ornamental rod is a mace.
5. The group still meets, but not in the same room as the one described here, which survived a major threat in 1605, but burned down in 1834.

page 18 ☚ Bonfire ☛ page 70

1. Rouen is a town in Normandy, in France. At the time of this scene, it was occupied by the English.
2. The girl led an army to victory against her enemies when she was only 17.
3. She carried a white banner with gold lilies embroidered on it into battle.
4. She was accused of being a witch and putting the King of France under her spell.
5. She was sold to her enemies for 10,000 pounds – a king's ransom in her day.

page 25 ☚ Cinders ☛ page 74

1. The man in the story is considered to have been a great man.
2. Several years later, when the woman found out who the man was, she was very embarrassed at how she'd behaved.
3. The story is said to have taken place in 876 CE and was first written down in 893 CE.
4. The man in the story eventually found a way to solve the problem he had with the Danes – and singing had something to do with it.
5. The scene took place on a small island in Somerset called Athelney, circled by the River Tone and the River Parrett. There's a monument there with an inscription that commemorates this story.
6. The man has a strong connection with Winchester. He's buried in the New Minster there, which he founded. There's a statue of him between the Broadway and the High Street by the British sculptor William (Hamo) Thornycroft that was put up there in 1901 – 1,000 years after he died.

page 23 ☚ Elephants ☛ page 78

1. The leader of the army comes from Carthage, in modern Tunisia.
2. They say that the wars this army has and will engage in are the largest, most savage wars ever fought up to then.
3. The leader's name literally means 'Baal is merciful to me'.
4. When it started out, this army had 38,000 infantry, 8,000 cavalry, and 37 African elephants.
5. The leader of the army is only 29 years old.

page 4 ☚ G ☛ page 81

1. The goldsmith's surname began with G.
2. It happened in the 1440s.
3. A vital factor in the success of this invention was that the first paper mill in Germany was opened in the 1390s.
4. Another vital factor in the success of this invention was the creation of a thick, oil-based ink.
5. The goldsmith went into this as a plan 'B' when investors who had wanted him to make concave metal mirrors to catch miraculous rays from relics that were exhibited to pilgrims every four years were thwarted when the pilgrimage for the following year was cancelled due to an outbreak of the plague. To get some return on their money, they decided to invest in this idea instead.
6. The patronage of the Catholic Church helped get this idea off the ground.
7. The invention was later instrumental in supporting the establishment of the Protestant Church.

page 14 ☚ Hoopoe ☛ page 83

1. Her story is told in the Bible, the Qur'an and the Ethiopian *Kebra Nagast* (The Glory of the Kings).
2. In the Arab world, she is called Bilkis.
3. The king is famous for many reasons – one of which is that

he built the first Jewish temple in Jerusalem.

4. The king is also thought to have written three books of the Old Testament.
5. The king's father was called David.

page 9 ☜ KKM ☞ page 87

1. The letters in the title of this riddle refer to three names.
2. The three structures are huge, but not equal in size.
3. One of these structures is the only one of the seven ancient wonders of the world that is still standing.
4. There are four letters in the name of the river mentioned in the riddle.
5. The rulers' names would have written in pictograms.

page 19 ☜ Life and Death ☞ page 89

1. The man was black.
2. He came from a royal family.
3. The speech was given on 20 April 1964 when the man was 45 years old.
4. He appeared in a cameo role in Spike Lee's 1992 film, *Malcolm X*.
5. A variety of things, including a species of woodpecker that lived around 3–5 million years ago, a nuclear particle, and a species of spider discovered in 2002 have been named after him.

page 12 ☜ Maps ☞ page 94

1. The king and queen are Catholic.
2. This happened in fourteen hundred and ninety-two.
3. The meeting took place in Córdoba.
4. The meeting took place in the Alcázar.
5. The man's forename and surname both start with the same letter.

page 10 ☚ Never Man ☛ page 95

1. The Chief Staff Officer was Hastings Lionel 'Pug' Ismay, 1st Baron Ismay.
2. The country has just come through a particularly period of heavy air attacks.
3. The older man is known for smoking cigars.
4. He is also known for his eloquence.
5. A few days before this event, the Germans had occupied most of France.

page 4 ☚ Pine Tree ☛ page 98

1. The writer and his uncle are both famous for their writing, although both had high-ranking jobs within the Roman administration in their day.
2. It happened in what we now know as the Bay of Naples.
3. The recipient was a senator who was also well-known as a writer.
4. The recipient's name means 'having been silent'.
5. The letter was written in Latin.

page 22 ☚ Revolt ☛ page 101

1. Julius Caesar crossed the stretch of water twice before and Caligula turned back before he even set out to cross it.
2. The scene happened where Boulogne is today.
3. The man who managed to change the army's mind was called Narcissus.

page 6 ☚ Revolution ☛ page 103

1. For nine years, the young woman taught art to the older woman's sister-in-law, Elisabeth, a member of the royal family. (Hint: we're talking about the French royal family here.)
2. The young woman has just been released from prison where she and her mother shared a cell with the woman

who was to become the future Empress Josephine.

3. Both women are famous. (Hint: the older one is famous mainly because of what she was; the younger one mainly because of what she did.)
4. The young woman will use the plaster cast to make a wax model of the older woman's head. (Hint: it will go on display in Paris and later in England.)
5. Both women have the same first name. (Hint: it's the French version of Mary.)

page 5 ☚ Sealed ☛ page 105

1. The man in purple robes is the Archbishop of Canterbury.
2. In the crowd with us are 25 noblemen, 20 monks, 12 church leaders apart from the king.
3. The barons want the king to put his seal on an important document, but they're not sure whether he's going to agree to or not.
4. The name of the field we're in is derived from two Anglo-Saxon words: *runieg* (a regular meeting) and *mede* (a meadow).
5. The King is called King John.
6. As far as I know, Robin Hood isn't among the people.

page 8 ☚ Shells ☛ page 112

1. The emperor's name literally means 'little boot'.
2. The emperor had a famous horse called Incitatus.
3. The emperor made his horse, Incitatus, a priest and wanted to make Incitatus a consul as well.
4. The emperor was Mark Anthony's great-grandson.
5. The army was following a trail that Julius Caesar had laid first in 55 BCE then in 54 BCE.

page 17 ☚ Stand Up! ☛ page 116

1. The woman's forename is the Italian name of a flower.

2. The woman's surname is a word you'd use to describe open green spaces.
3. The woman was black.
4. The incident happened in December 1955.
5. The incident happened in Montgomery, Alabama.

page 11 ☚ Stars ☛ page 123

1. One of the men is her uncle-in-law; the other is a colonel in the army.
2. The shape she has just cut out of paper is a five-pointed star.
3. The woman's given name is Elizabeth, but she's better known by a shorter version of that name.
4. The house described in the riddle is still standing today. It's been made into a museum.
5. As a result of the commission, the woman came to be thought of as a national heroine.
6. The woman was a Quaker.

page 16 ☚ Stop! ☛ page 126

1. The man who appears as a victim in this story was a captain.
2. The saviour was the chieftain's daughter.
3. There are four syllables in the woman's name.
4. The man and the woman are featured in a song that Peggy Lee, Ella Fitzgerald, and Elvis Presley recorded, not to be confused with one of the same name which Lady Gaga recorded.
5. The scene took place at Werowocomoco, near Jamestown, Virginia.

page 13 ☚ Terrible Twos ☛ page 127

1. The king was visited and not visited by three wise men before this happened.

2. This happened in the same town in which Jesus was born.
3. The fact that the king only ordered the killing of male children is significant.

page 7 ☚ Time! ☛ page 131

1. The scene took place in Plymouth.
2. The man who suggested they finish the game was known as 'the dragon' and had a price on his head of 20,000 ducats.
3. He's famous for 'singeing the King of Spain's beard'.
4. He was the first English man to see the Pacific Ocean.
5. He was the first English man to circumnavigate the globe and the second European to do so.

page 28 ☚ Torches ☛ page 132

1. The philosopher had just returned from Campania, in the Bay of Naples, where an earthquake had struck on 5 February 63 CE.
2. A couple of years later, the emperor travelled to Greece to take part in the Olympic Games of 65 CE as a wrestler. He lost, but was announced the winner for diplomatic reasons and returned to Rome in triumph.
3. The emperor's mother was called Agrippina. She was the most powerful Roman woman in the entire history of the Roman Empire.

page 24 ☚ Travellers' Tales ☛ page 133

1. The travellers had been away for so long, people back home had assumed they'd died abroad. When they returned from their travels, they were dressed so shabbily and spoke so strangely that no one recognised them, not even their own family.
2. The house is called a *palazzo* in the local dialect.
3. The storyteller's favourite word is 'millions'.

4. The cathedral is dedicated to St Mark, after whom the storyteller in our tale is named.
5. The merchant did end up writing a book which influenced map-making and discovery for centuries after. Christopher Columbus, for one, took it with him when he set out on his voyage of discovery in 1492.

page 3 ☚ Vision ☛ page 140

1. The man, whose real name was Tatanka Iyotake, was a member of a Native American tribe.
2. The event took place in 1875. Three years earlier, during the Battle of Arrow Creek, the man had performed a legendary act of bravery, by walking out into the space between the two hostile parties, lighting a peace pipe, smoking it, cleaning it out and returning to his side, while bullets bounced around him, threatening to end his life at any moment.
3. The event took place in the Black Hills area of North America.
4. The assembled company had just participated together in a ritual Sun Dance.
5. Nine years after this event, the man toured America and Europe in a show called Buffalo Bill's Wild West, in which he featured as a star performer.

page 27 ☚ Webs ☛ page 143

1. The story was one of many such first published under the title of *Tales of a Grandfather* in 1827.
2. Edinburgh's main railway station is named after a fictional character this writer created.
3. Some say the writer created the character traits of Robin Hood as we know him today.
4. The writer is famous for books such as the *Waverley Novels*, which include *Rob Roy*, *Ivanhoe* and *Kenilworth*.

5. The king in the story asked his best friend to have the king's heart removed after his death and take it to the Holy Land so that even though his body could not be brought there, his heart might make it.

Background information

I've mentioned this in the introductory notes, but just in case you missed it, in this section, the background information to the riddles is arranged by title in alphabetical order. Each title is followed by a brief description of the subject of the riddle in italics, followed by a more in-depth exploration of the characters and themes involved. This is followed by a short bibliographical essay with suggestions for further reading. The essays refer to articles, books and online resources (A#, B# and C# respectively – think of 'C' as standing for 'Cyberspace'). The hash tag here stands for a number in the respective section in the bibliography which starts on page [pp].

15

Rome, 44 BCE—The assassination of Julius Caesar.

This scene depicts the last hours of Julius Caesar's life and aims to give an overview of his achievements. The story continues in the room in which the senate of Rome are meeting that day. Inside, Caesar greets the assembled senators and calls the meeting to order. First up is a senator called Metellus Cimber. He wants Caesar to allow his brother who's living in exile to be allowed back in to Rome. The scroll in Cimber's hand is presented to Caesar. Caesar reaches forward to take it. As he does so, he feels a pull on his toga. The forceful, violent move makes it fall off his shoulder and he calls out. He tries to rise … he feels something sharp digging into his neck. He stops to look round. He sees senator Publius Casca holding a dagger. Caesar thrusts him to one side and the dagger falls. Caesar is no stranger to having to defend himself, but he's unarmed. Another dagger presses into him from the other side. It's Casca's brother, Gaius. Caesar turns. Sixty daggers in the hands of the assembled senators face him. Caesar shouts out, tries to break through – but the powerful emperor, polymath, poet, powerless in the face of raw hatred and violence, falls. Thirty-one stab wounds would be enough to kill most people. Caesar's still alive. Then the senator whom Caesar has always thought of as his son approaches him – he might even be his son, you know, since his mother was Caesar's mistress for a while – and Caesar calls out, "Brutus!" and Brutus adds his blow to the others, knifing Caesar in the balls. Caesar drapes his toga over his face to veil the sight of his assassins from his eyes. He falls to the floor. Dead. Brutus pauses; rises; makes to address the senate, but then runs out. The other conspirators follow him. The news breaks – "Caesar's dead!" The crowds rush in from the street and bring Caesar's body out.

The man in the scene who wanted to stop Caesar entering the building is Mark Antony, a close family friend and, as Master of the Horse, the holder of a high-ranking military position. He'd heard about the plot to assassinate Caesar and had wanted to stop him from entering the senate. He'd been barred from approaching Caesar by a group of senators who were part of the conspiracy. Hoping against hope that Caesar had avoided death, Mark Antony has waited outside. Now, when he sees Brutus and the other senators emerging, proudly waving their bloodstained daggers, he turns and runs, leaving the city disguised as a slave. Later, he comes back and addresses the people, incites them to hunt down the remaining conspirators and gets himself elected consul. Among other things, Mark Antony is famous for becoming Cleopatra's lover after Caesar's death.

Explore further

This riddle and the background information to it are based on accounts in Suetonius' *Life of Caesar* (B121 – Book 1, Chapters 81/2 – pp 106–113) and Plutarch's *Life of Caesar* and *Life of Brutus* (B93 – Chapters 62–68 and Chapters 8–18 – Volume 6, pp 586–605 and pp 140–167 respectively). From there, you might enjoy exploring other treatments of the story, such as Shakespeare's *Julius Caesar*,

Thornton Wilder's *The Ides of March* (B145), or one of the many films which feature Caesar's assassination, from Mankiewicz's *Cleopatra* (1963) starring Elizabeth Taylor, Rex Harrison and Richard Burton to the English camp comedy, *Carry on Cleo* (1964) starring Amanda Barrie as Cleopatra, Kenneth Williams as Julius Caesar and Sid James as Mark Antony.

A Photo Shoot?!

Ekaterinburg, Russia, 17 July 1918—The assassination of Tsar Nicholas II and his family.

This account is based on the first-hand report given by Anatolie Alexandrovitch Yakimoff, a 31-year-old workman who was one of a group of 10 factory workers hired to guard the Russian royal family in May 1918.

The roots of the story lie in the period leading up to the First World War. The extension of the Trans-Siberian Railway to Vladivostok and the abolition of serfdom in the nineteenth century extended geographical and psychological horizons for people across Russia. In real terms, however, the old restrictive regimes lingered on in different guises and financial crises hit practical aspirations hard. Russia was not faring well in its war with Japan. Strikes in 1904 led to protests in 1905, which were quashed by force by the ruling powers. On 22 January 1905, a group of unarmed protesters were fired upon in what came to be known as the Bloody Sunday massacre. Plans to assassinate the Tsar's uncle, the Grand Duke Sergei, were finally carried out on 17 February 1905.

The unrest continued, however. Crew members on the Battleship Potemkin mutinied in June 1905. Eventually the situation stabilised after the adoption of the October Manifesto which greatly decreased imperial power.

As the years progressed, Russia gradually found itself embroiled in the events that led to the outbreak of the First World War. As the war progressed, there was a growing dissatisfaction with the Tsar's incompetence as military leader at the front; and at home, with the empress's blind faith in the 'holy fool' Rasputin. The growing levels of dissatisfaction led to massed protests in Russia in February 1917. On 15 March, Tsar Nicholas II abdicated in favour of his brother, the Grand Duke Michael. The Grand Duke declined to take up the throne in the circumstances unless his appointment was based on a referendum that found for monarchy (rather than a republic) as a legitimate form of government. This left the power in the hands of a Provisional Government.

The actions of the Provisional Government in relation to the royal family smack of fear and unease in the legitimacy of their position. Despite that, the reasons for the assassination of the royal family remain unclear. The Provisional Government had publicly proposed that the Tsar be put on trial. However, concerned that the Romanovs would provide a rallying point for those opposed to the Provisional Government; and under hostile threat from forces with superior numbers of fighters, they moved the royal family away from Moscow, rather than to the capital city, and put them in the care of the Bolshevik party in power in Ekaterinburg.

At first, it was only Tsar Nicholas II, the Empress Maria Feodorovna and their daughter Maria who were moved from Tobolsk to the Ipatiev House in Ekaterinburg in April 1918. In May, the Tsarevich Alexei and his sisters Olga, Tatiana and Anastasia joined them. The young Tsarevich had been unwell and had stayed in Tobolsk with his three sisters until he recovered and was well enough for all of them to make the journey north-west to join their sister and parents.

Anatolie heard the story of the assassination from Klescheeff, one of his fellow guards. According to his account, the jewels, hidden in the women's corsets, amounting to 1.3 kilos in weight, acted as a defensive shield against the assassins' bullets, only serving to delay the inevitable and prolong the agony of the event. The jewels ended up in a pile on the table in the guards' room; the bodies, buried secretly in unmarked graves. Their dog, surviving, searched the house for them following their deaths.

Anatolie believed that the bodies had all been buried together. However, investigations in 1979 and in 2007 revealed two burial sites had been used. In 1981, Tsar Nicholas II and his family were recognised as martyred saints in the Russian Orthodox Church Outside Russia. In 1998, the recovered remains were given a state burial and laid to rest in the Cathedral of Saint Peter and Saint Paul in St Petersburg. In 2000, they were canonised as passion-bearers by the Orthodox Church in Russia. In 2008, the Supreme Court of the Russian Federation ruled that the royal family should be 'rehabilitated', in an attempt to undo a history of negative Soviet propaganda that had been associated with the last of the Romanovs to rule Russia. The reversal arguably did less good than the invitation to consider a more open-ended, balanced interpretation of events and achievements.

How Anatolie's sister would have taken it at the time is unclear from the transcript. While a reaction of horror at the atrocity of the deed on a purely human level would probably have prevailed, it is by no means certain. It would very much have depended on her personal values and religious and political views. The question regarding her reaction is provided as a starting point for debate as to what her views might have been if she had been, say, a passionate supporter of the Russian Orthodox Church; of the Bolsheviks; of the White Army; of the Red Army; or as a passionate liberal intellectual, to name some of the main demarcations of the time.

Yurovsky – who was in charge of security at the Ipatiev House and who was responsible for carrying out the order for the assassination – later became Chief of the Gold Department of the Soviet State Treasury. Towards the end of his life, he expressed concern about his elderly mother, "who does not share my views but who may suffer simply because I am her son."

Robert Wilton, clearly sympathetic to the royalist cause and understandably moved by the injustice of the murders, adds that she 'feared and loathed her son'.

Anatolie's account includes an account of the personalities of his superiors, of the people who worked at the Ipatiev House, and of his fellow guards, as well as an account of Yurovsky's background.

The account shows a shift in Anatolie's attitude towards the royal family. Observed at close quarters, their humanity and deportment cause him to say, "After I personally saw them several times I began to feel entirely different towards them: I began to pity them. I pitied them as human beings … Previously, when I first entered into the guards, I did not see them and did not know them."

Behind this riddle lie two basic questions: How can we, through studying the dynamic forces behind the event, move beyond fear, loathing, pity, and empathy to a wider discussion of the issue of the taking of life? And how can we then move from an integrated instinctive, imaginative, knowledge-based starting point, to the realisation of an integrated form of social action as a result?

Explore further

Anatolie's report was recorded as part of the investigation conducted in July 1918 by the Siberian government into the assassination of the royal family (B124).

Primary sources, including Alexander II's Manifesto of February 19 1861 abolishing serfdom in Russia (C3) and a map of the Trans-Siberian railway dating from 1903 (C1) can be found on line as can several articles: Richard Cavendish's article in *History Today* on the 'Bloody Sunday' massacre (A7), and accounts of the Romanovs' elevation to sainthood (A1, C8) and their rehabilitation (C6).

For more in-depth overviews of the socio-political events

which led up to the assassination of Tsar Nicholas and his family, see Richard Pipes' *The Russian Revolution* (B91). For further details on Rasputin and his influence on the Empress Alexandra, see Edvard Radzinsky's *Rasputin: The Last Word* (B100). For an exploration of the phenomenon of the 'holy fool' in Russia, see EM Thompson's *Understanding Russia: The Holy Fool in Russian Culture* (B126). Information on the decision to bring the Romanovs to trial can be found in Helen Rappaport's *Ekaterinburg: The Last Days of the Romanovs* (B102) and Steinberg and Khrustalëv's *The Fall of the Romanovs* (B117). Details of the search for the remains of the tsar and his family can be found in Wendy Slater's *The Many Deaths of Tsar Nicholas II* (B116).

Asp

Alexandria, 30 BCE—Cleopatra, the last pharaoh of Ancient Egypt takes her own life.

Cleopatra's life – and death – have inspired countless accounts and artistic works over the last two millennia. Not surprising, with reports of how the last queen of Egypt smuggled herself into Caesar's presence rolled up in a carpet featuring in accounts of her life, not to mention the tragic, yet romantic circumstances of her death.

The lover of two Roman emperors, the ruler of Egypt, subject to extremes of emotions – the paradoxical nature of this and many other events in her life reveal a highly unusual, individual, and complex character.

Was she a seductive temptress whom men found impossible to resist, or a highly intelligent and powerful woman who was the equal of men such as Caesar? Was she dangerously manipulative or charmingly appealing? Or perhaps all of the above – however she is seen, there is a common thread of guarded admiration in writers' accounts of Cleopatra's life.

The facts are that Cleopatra was a strategist who took her role as ruler seriously. When Egypt faced poverty and famine, arising from a severe drought and compounded by extreme debt to Rome incurred by her father, she issued decrees that helped Egypt get through the crisis. All the more impressive, when you learn that she issued them when she was 18 years old.

She died 21 years later, aged 39. The version of the story on which this riddle is based comes from Plutarch. In this version, Antony, defeated by Octavian, and hearing a report that Cleopatra had killed herself, gave his dagger to his slave, Eros, and asked Eros to kill him. Eros, however, turned the dagger on himself rather than kill his master. Antony, not wanting to be outdone by his slave, stabbed himself in the gut, just as the queen's secretary, Diomedes, appeared to tell Antony that she was still alive and had shut herself in her mausoleum to protect herself from being captured by Octavian. Antony immediately asked to be carried to her. According to Plutarch, the mausoleum had windows on the first floor, through which the fatally wounded Mark Antony was hauled. He died in her arms.

The precise location of Cleopatra's mausoleum is still unknown. Plutarch's *Life of Antony* locates it in a coastal city, with hills in front of it. This topographical detail suggests that it was not in Alexandria, a relatively flat city where Cleopatra had her palace. Rather, archaeologists have conjectured recently that it may have been at Toposiris Magna. The building is described as having a door at ground level, thin enough to allow those outside to converse with those inside when it was closed. According to Cassius Dio, Cleopatra was able to look out over the top of the edifice.

It is a few days after Antony's death that Plutarch and Dio describe Cleopatra, then Octavian's prisoner, taking her own life. As to how, Strabo mentions that she might have killed herself by using a poisonous ointment, but the version that has stood the test of time is that she was bitten by an asp (or more likely a cobra) hiding in a basket of figs. Plutarch and Dio put forward additional theories – that the serpent was hiding in a water jar, which she poked and prodded about in with a golden distaff until it leapt up and bit her; or that it was hidden in a bunch of flowers; or that she pricked herself with a poisoned comb. Plutarch and Dio also mention that before dying, Cleopatra sent a message to Suetonius, asking that she and Antony be buried together. Dio and Suetonius have Octavian sending her help, when he found out she'd tried to commit suicide, but failing to stop her death. Unable to carry her to Rome alive to take part in his triumphal procession, according to Plutarch, Octavian ordered an image of her to be made, complete with asp – arguably the most visibly powerful and obvious of the symbols that could have been used – which he paraded through the streets of Rome, along with a huge proportion of Egypt's wealth which he finally annexed, something Julius Caesar had seen fit not to do. The procession would have been seen by crowds of people, many of whom would have remembered seeing her from her stay there between 46–44 BCE, obviously Caesar's lover.

It is arguable that it is as much the visual aspect of the serpent, which has made it endure as the means of Cleopatra's death, as the symbolic aspect of it – it was one of the symbols used by Egyptian royalty to symbolise transcendence through a unification of opposites, a fitting symbol of Cleopatra's claim to immortal fame, which transcends the limitations of life to allow the story of her death to continue to live on and inspire us to this day.

Her story lives on in Hollywood biopics and television documentaries, and new archaeological digs continue to reveal further details about her life and times.

Explore further

The main classical accounts of Cleopatra come from Plutarch's *Life of Antony* and *Life of Caesar* (B93 – Chapters 76–87 and Chapter 49 – Volume 9, pp 309–331 and Volume 7, pp 558/9 respectively), Cassius Dio Cocceianus' *Roman History* (B25 – Book

51, Chapter 10 – Volume 6, pp 28–31), Strabo's *Geography* (B119 – Book 7, Chapter 1, Line 10) and Suetonius' *Life of Caesar* (B121 – Book 2, Chapter 17 – Volume 2, pp 146–147). Other Classical writers, such as Appian (B4 – Book 5, Chapter 1 – Volume 4, pp 366–367), Horace (B49 – Ode 37, Book 1 – pp 38/39), Lucan (B67 – Book 10), Virgil (B135 – Book 8, Lines 671–728), Propertius (B98 – Book 3, Elegy 11, line 39 – p 113) were less favourable towards her. The latter refers to Cleopatra as the 'harlot queen of polluted Canopus'.

You may wish to compare the classical biographies by male historians with later readings of their accounts of Cleopatra's life by women, including Edith Flamarion (B36), Joann Fletcher (B37), Stacy Schiff (B114) and Joyce Tyldesley (B131).

A good starting point to find out more information about the context in which Cleopatra ruled is DJ Thompson's *Cleopatra VII: The Queen in Egypt* (A47). A good starting point to explore the (for some, controversial) world of symbolist Egyptology, particularly with reference to the role of the serpent, see John Anthony West's *Serpent in the Sky* (B142). For information about the excavation of her tomb, see the articles and videos on the BBC News website (C5, C69) and *Cleopatra: The Search for the Last Queen of Egypt* by Franck Goddio and Zahi Hawass, covering details of the National Geographic exhibition which toured the US in 2011/12 (B45). A particularly good fictional account of her stay in Egypt can be found in Thornton Wilder's *The Ides of March* (B145). You may also wish to compare the characterisation of Cleopatra in Shakespeare's *Antony and Cleopatra* with George Bernard Shaw's treatment in his play, *Caesar and Cleopatra*.

Bang!

Martin Luther nails a copy of his 95 theses to the door of All Saints' Church, Wittenberg in 1517. The theses are distributed in print across Europe, reaching Pope Leo X, who issues a rebuttal in the form of a papal bull known as the Exsurge Domine (*Arise, O Lord*) *in 1520.*

Martin Luther's act of nailing a copy of his theses to the door of All Saints' Church is widely seen as the start of the reformation. Did it all start with the theses? Well, they didn't come out of thin air. As CM Jacobs outlines, it all started with plans by Pope Julius II (Giuliano della Rovere, known as *il Papa terribile* – The Terrible Pope) to do something with the marble that one of his predecessors (Pope Nicholas V, Tommaso Parentucelli, who had been pope during the fall of Constantinople in 1453) had taken from the Coliseum in order to use to restore St Peter's Basilica in Rome. Nothing had been done about the restoration project due to conflicts between popes in Rome and Avignon, and the old basilica had fallen into disrepair. The piles of marble had been lying there for over half a century. Julius decided to knock the old basilica down and build a fitting contemporary Renaissance monument that would celebrate God and the Catholic Church. To raise funds for the project, he issued a special *Jubilee Indulgence* in 1503, extending it in 1510, offering people forgiveness for their sins and offering their souls freedom from purgatory if they met certain conditions, including confession and pilgrimage. He died before the project could be completed. He was succeeded by Pope Leo X (Giovanni Lorenzo de' Medici), who took on the responsibility of seeing the project realised, and raising the necessary funds to do so. One of the ways he did this was to issue indulgences and accept incentives from ambitious clerics. One such cleric was Albrecht von Brandenburg, the younger brother of the Elector of Brandenburg at the time. Albrecht had already been appointed archbishop of Magdeburg in 1513 at the age of 23, although officially, the youngest a bishop was supposed to be was 27. Not content with presiding over one diocese, even though he was 'under age', he asked the Pope for the right to preside over two. The negotiations were conducted via the Fuggers, a rich merchant banking family. The Fuggers informed Albrecht that the Pope would be willing to look leniently on his request if a sum of 1,000 ducats for each of the twelve Apostles was offered to the church. Albrecht offered 7,000 for the seven deadly sins. They settled on 10,000, a sum which did *not* relate to the Ten Commandments, according to Bainton, but who knows? Albrecht did not have that kind of money lying around, but thought it was a sum worth paying. He borrowed money from the Fuggers, who agreed to lend the bishop the money on the condition that he would pay them back through the exclusive sale of the special indulgences in his dioceses, with 50 per cent of the proceeds going to the Vatican (in addition to the sum already received by the Holy See) and 50 per cent to the Fuggers. To get the deal to work and ensure he didn't lose the opportunity to add a significant sum to the credit side of the double entry register relating to the Vatican's great building project he'd taken so much to heart, Pope Leo X revived the jubilee indulgence. If you lived in the diocese of Magdeburg, in which Wittenberg lay, you had to travel to a neighbouring diocese to receive an indulgence. Brandenburg was the diocese of choice. Once there, you were likely to be uplifted by the eloquence of a Dominican monk, Johann Tetzel, who spun such stories of the benefits of buying indulgences from him that he was suspended from the priesthood by the Papal Nuncio and Legate to the Elector of Saxony, Frederick the Wise in 1518.

While authors agree on the general features of the picture painted, their accounts vary in terms of details such as the amounts paid by Albrecht to the Vatican, or owed to the Fuggers. Schaff notes that Albrecht paid the Vatican 10,000 ducats 'with sundry additions' for three sees, amounting to a total of more than 30,000 ducats, and ended up owing the Fuggers 30,000 florins. Häberlein puts the total amount Albrecht owed the Fuggers at 48,000 florins, of which he was able to repay 42,000 from the sale of indulgences.

It was this trade in indulgences that caused a mass exodus of parishioners out of Wittenberg, where Luther was based, and neither the exodus nor the reasons behind it were neutrally observed by Luther. Luther had been thinking hard about penitence for a while – he had preached sermons in 1516 and 1517 which argued that indulgences could not offer a guarantee of salvation, at least not without true penitence. He had been embroiled in theological debates within the theological faculty at the University of Wittenberg with Archdeacon Andreas Karlstadt. In a heated debate, Luther challenged his colleague to disprove that earlier scholastic theologians had misunderstood both scripture and Augustine. As a result of the debate, Karlstadt came round to Luther's way of thinking and, on 26 April 1517, published 151 theses which Luther read and liked. Luther was finishing a commentary on the seven penitential psalms (Psalms 6, 32, 38, 52, 102, 130, 143) which was published that year and on the eve of All Saints' Day 1517 (now celebrated as Halloween), Luther wrote to both his own bishop and Archbishop Karlstadt, outlining his concerns about the way in which salvation was being sold and enclosing a copy of his theses.

Did he also nail them up on the door of All Saints' Church? Those who argue that he did cite that this was normal practice and that public theological debates were announced this way. They point out that the story appears in Melancthon's biography. Critics point out that it doesn't appear in Luther's autobiography, that Melancthon may not have been in Wittenberg at the time and that it has become the stuff of legend, with no known basis for fact.

However, Melancthon states that the theses were nailed up on the eve of All Saints' Day. The late Professor Junghans notes that the date coincided that year with the opening of the church for veneration of the vast collection of relics amassed by Frederick III, Elector of Saxony, with whom the All Saints castle church (as opposed to the town church of St Mary) was associated. By 1520 the collection comprised 19,023 holy objects, including a relic of the crown of thorns, a bit of the burning bush in front of which Moses had stood, soot from the furnace in which Shadrach,

Meshach and Abednego had been placed, and the remains of one of the holy innocents slain by King Herod. The veneration, Junghans claims, was linked to an indulgence known as the *portiuncula indulgence*. This was an indulgence originally granted to St Francis in 1221 by Pope Honorius III. The indulgence was extended to the castle church in 1398 to be granted to all who visited the castle church to attend confession and venerate the relics there between 31 October and 1 November – the eve and day of the Feast of All Saints, to whom the church was dedicated.

Did he? Didn't he? Personally, I lean towards oral history, tempered by historical research, and so far, the case against is not convincing enough for me to label the story as spurious. If it is proved to be so one day, then Bang! goes another historical legend. Until then, let's bang on about it!

Explore further

The history of the reformation goes beyond Martin Luther and the question of indulgences. It involves political and doctrinal issues, as well as questions of spiritual and temporal power, the management of ecclesiastical resources and much more. For more information, see Euan Cameron's *The European Reformation* (B18), Michael Mullett's *The Catholic Reformation* (B81), Steven Ozment's *The Age of Reform: 1250–1550: An Intellectual and Religious History of Late Medieval and Reformation Europe* (B86), and Professor Peter Wallace's *The Long European Reformation: Religion, Political Conflict, and the Search for Conformity, 1350–1750* (B140).

Narrowing the focus to Luther himself, the two main primary sources for his life are his autobiography (B68) and the biography by his friend and colleague, Philipp Melanchthon (B78). For further sources, see David Whitford's *Reformation and Early Modern Europe: A Guide to Research* (B144).

Two good places to start if you want to find out more about Martin Luther are CM Jacobs' *Works of Martin Luther with Introductions and Notes* (B53) and Roland Bainton's *Here I Stand: A*

Life of Martin Luther (B7). Luther's *Letter to the Archbishop of Mainz, 1517*, can be found in Jacobs (B53 – Volume 1, pp 24–28) and on line (C47). A good online source for Luther's own works is the directory at lutherdansk.dk.

Information on Fugger's deals can be found in the Schaffs' *History of the Christian Church* (B113 – Volume 5, Part 2, pp 764/5), the chapter on *Business with the Roman Curia* in Mark Häberlein's *The Fuggers of Augsburg* (B40) and John Hartwig's *Jakob Fugger and his Influence on the Reformation* (C33).

Archbishop Albrecht von Brandenburg's *Instructions Relating to the Conditions of the Sale of Indulgences in Germany (Instructio summaria ad Subcommissarios Poenitentiarum et Confessores)* are published in Hans Hillerbrand's *The Reformation* (B47 – pp 37–41). For more information on him, see Christopher Rees's *Pyrrhic Victory: The Disputation at Pleissenburg Castle* (C63); Helmar Junghans' *Luther's Wittenberg* (A25); William Kent's article on *Indulgences* (A27); and PMJ Rock's article on *Canonical Age* (A39), in *The Catholic Encyclopedia*.

The history of the Frederick the Wise's collection of relics can be found in Holger Klein's essay in the exhibition catalogue for *Treasures of Heaven: Saints, Relics, and Devotion in Medieval Europe* (A28). Shadrach, Meshach and Abednego were three wise, high-ranking Jews in Babylon who refused to bow down to King Nebuchadnezzar's golden idol. He ordered them to be thrown into a burning, fiery furnace, from which they emerged unscathed. Their story can be found in the Old Testament Book of Daniel, Chapters 1–3.

Bees

Paris, 2 December 1804—Napoleon's coronation as Emperor of the French at Notre Dame Cathedral in the presence of the Pope.

Napoleon's coronation ceremony is particularly notable for its merging of two historic ceremonies – the French royal coronation ceremony and the papal imperial coronation ceremony, with appropriate innovations introduced, reflecting the ethos of the French Republic in 1792 which abolished the constitutional monarchy in France, yet, paradoxically drew on the traditional coronation rites of the very monarchic system it had abolished in order to establish its legitimacy.

The coronation ceremony was clearly influenced by Charlemagne's legacy, as was Napoleon's separate coronation as King of Italy, with a significant difference – whereas Charlemagne had gone to the Pope to be crowned, Napoleon had the Pope come to him.

The presence of the Pope 'on away territory' was significant, particularly in light of the Concordat of 1801 which set out to reformulate the relationship between the Catholic Church and the newly formed French political system. At once a conciliatory document, which brought together church and state in many ways, it also laid the foundation for the later break of church and state in 1905.

The points at which church and state merged and split in the early days of the French Empire were clearly marked in Napoleon's coronation ceremony. On the one hand, the presence of the Pope, the cathedral setting, the liturgical rite, the anointing with chrism, the consecration of regalia all show a clear link between sacred and secular. On the other hand, Napoleon's insistence on crowning himself, the setting of the enthronement at the west end of the cathedral – the farthest removed from the altar, and the Pope's withdrawal during Napoleon's reading the oath which bound the Emperor to uphold a legal code in which divorce was allowed and which allowed the disposal of church property all pointed to instances where the contemporary articulations of the sacred and the secular parted ways. The altar was set at a markedly lower height than the dais under the triumphal arch erected specially for the enthronement ceremony, for instance.

In seeking symbolic roots for the new order in older traditions, the organizers of the ceremony drew on the Imperial Eagle and chose to replace the familiar *fleur de lys* which had been associated with the kings and queens of France with an earlier royal emblem, based on bee-shaped ornaments found in the tomb of the Frankish king, Childeric I. Childeric died in 481 CE. His son, Clovis I, founded the Merovingian dynasty, which gave way to the Carolingian monarchy, from which Charlemagne, one of Napoleon's heroes, emerged.

Two months prior to his coronation, Napoleon visited the cathedral at Aachen (Aix-le-Chapelle), where Charlemagne had been buried and where relics relating to his coronation and anointing were carried before Bonaparte in procession. The Empress Josephine had preceded him there, on an official visit which had been planned as a result of Napoleon having been declared emperor. The occasion, according to one eyewitness, left him visibly moved.

Whether Childeric's bees were actually bees, or whether they were originally supposed to depict cicadas is a moot point. Napoleon's designers, however, clearly saw them as bees, and their inclusion was a conscious decision to include references to the early roots from which the monarchy developed in France.

Napoleon's coronation provided an excuse for lavish celebrations which lasted over several days. One of the most interesting showpieces, which turned out to have a twist of irony in the end, was the launch of a hot air balloon to commemorate the event. The balloon was still in the relatively early days of development. The launch was overseen by André-Jacques Garnerin, the first Official Aeronaut of France who expected it to float a few hundred metres and land in the French countryside. As the balloon was unmanned, he'd attached a note to it asking whoever found it to send word to him so he could come and pick it up. He little expected an answer to come from Rome. While the imperial connotations were favourable, the fact that the balloon had brushed against the tomb of Nero during its descent leaving the detached crown hanging there at a rakish angle was far less favourable. Napoleon was not at all pleased and decided instead to work with one of the first female aeronauts, Sophie Blanchard, after that.

As for Napoleon's height, he was at least 1 m 68.6 cm tall, according to the measurements taken of his body by the physician who was in attendance after his death, Dr Antonmarchi. As Dunan points out, he was sometimes depicted as diminutive by cartoonists such as Cruikshank for the purposes of political satire, in very much the same way as Mikheil Saakashvili is alleged to have called Vladimir Putin 'Lili-Putin' – a story which he has denied, yet which continues to circulate despite his denials.

Explore further

The scene in this riddle is based on the printed text of Napoleon's coronation ceremony (B1), the primary source account by FN Dusaulchoy (B33) and the detailed historical account by Frédéric Masson (B73). See also Peter Hicks' article, *Napoleon's Consecration and Coronation*, on the Fondation Napoléon website (C35) and Reginald Woolley's book on Coronation Rites (B149). An English translation of Napoleon's Concordat can be found on the Concordat Watch website (C32).

For the links between Napoleon and Charlemagne, see Thierry Lentz's article on this on the Fondation Napoléon website (C43). You can decide for yourself whether Childeric's 'bees' were bees or cicadas – they're illustrated on page 141 of Chifflet's work (B23). And digital reproductions of contemporary engravings of the enthronement area as it appeared on the day can be found on the Bridgeman website, www.bridgemanart.com, reference numbers UIG543744, STC129843, and UIG543798. Reference numbers for depictions of the coronation area LLM655417, LLM725975, and MAM714147.

You can also find out more about early balloon flights and the specific fate of the balloon that Garnerin launched to celebrate Napoleon's coronation in a radio programme by John Lienhard (C44) and in Louis Constant Wairy's *Recollections of the private life of Napoleon* (B139 – Volume 1, pp 313–317). A full account of the festivities held to celebrate the coronation is given by Dusaulchoy (B33).

A discussion about the measurement of Napoleon's height can be found in Marcel Dunan's article on the Fondation Napoléon website (A11). Cruikshank's cartoon is viewable on Wikimedia (C23). There's also a rather crude picture of a chamber pot – which is potentially as amusing as it is offensive – by an anonymous maker containing a figure of Napoleon in a *History Today* magazine blog review of the 2010 exhibition, *Rude Britannia* (C22). As for Putin and Saakashvili, you can follow their story by taking a look at Clifford Levy's article on the *New York Times* website (A31) and the anonymous report on the Civil Georgia website (C7).

Blast!

London, 4 November 1605—Guy Fawkes prepares to execute the 'Gunpowder Plot' – a plot to blow up the Palace of Westminster during the State Opening of Parliament.

Across the road from the site of the old Palace of Westminster in London lies Westminster Abbey. In the easternmost part of the Abbey, lies a chapel commissioned by Henry VII in honour of the Virgin Mary, called the Lady Chapel. To the right, as you enter, lies the funerary monument of the Catholic queen, Mary Tudor; to the left, that of the Protestant queen, Elizabeth I. Situated between them is a commemorative floor stone which reads,

> Near the tomb of Mary and Elizabeth remember before God all those who divided at the reformation by different convictions laid down their lives for Christ and conscience' sake

At the heart of the Guy Fawkes story lies a conflict between two views of what was true. It was a truth that determined the fate of your immortal soul, a truth for which people were willing to die, a truth for which people were willing to condemn others to death. And the tragedy is that these two views of truth were so divergent, neither party accepted the other was right, and neither accepted that neither can have been truly true. And what was that truth? It was the truth of the 'one true religion'.

It was a battle of beliefs; a fight for faith. The war that was waged in defence of this truth was more than a war of words; it was a war fought with wounds, with blood, with lives. And Guy Fawkes had decided to use an act of terrorism to fight for what he believed was true.

Born in 1570, he converted from Anglicanism to Catholicism when he was 18, in the year in which the Spanish Armada was defeated. In his early twenties, with pressure on English Catholics rising, he sold his property in England and followed other dissatisfied English Catholics to the Continent. There, on religious grounds, he fought on the side of Catholic Spain against the Protestant Netherlands. Then he fought against France in a conflict that culminated in the *Treaty of Nantes*, which declared support for freedom of conscience and distinguished between the need for civil unity and religious unity. It seemed that this concession did not satisfy Guy Fawkes, who may well have believed that both were not just vital, but worth fighting – and potentially dying – for.

At first he had tried negotiation. He had been active in prolonged acts of diplomacy and negotiation with King Philip of Spain in 1603, which had not had the result he had hoped for.

At 34, he returned to England, to work with a group of Catholics to get rid of the major barrier to the restoration of Catholicism to England – by whatever means it took.

What was he fighting back against? The imposition of Protestant beliefs. Who did this group see as the main culprit?

King James I of England and VI of Scotland and his parliament, who were passing a growing number of Acts against Recusancy of increasing severity.

It was a story that had started in England with Henry VIII's break with the Catholic Church. After Mary I had returned to Catholicism, Elizabeth I swung the country back to Protestantism, instituting a series of measures to restrict Catholics from holding offices, from higher education, starting with two acts passed in 1559: the *Act of Supremacy* (1 Eliz. 1) and the *Act of Uniformity* (1 Eliz. 2). The first required anyone who took up a public or church office to vow allegiance to the state and risk being fined, having their property confiscated and titles (where relevant) revoked, and being convicted of treason if they refused, the punishment for which was to be hung, drawn, and quartered. This provoked a crisis of conscience for English Catholics. The second act required all people to attend weekly church services which followed the Church of England rite. In 1581, the *Act Against Reconciliation to Rome* (23 Eliz. 1 c. 1) raised the fine for recusancy, which had been 12 pence per non-attendance (a prohibitive sum for the poor) to 20 pounds a month and imposed punishments of imprisonment for non-payment (until the money was paid) and imprisonment for those who celebrated or attended mass. The 1593 *Act Against Seditious Sectaries* (35 Eliz. 1 c. 1) and the *Popish Recusants Act* (35 Eliz. 1 c. 2) forced many young Catholics into exile, and restricted those who remained staunchly Catholic to a 5-mile radius of their houses. With the accession of James I, there was hope of a more lenient policy of toleration. This was, indeed, practised, until the unfolding of the Bye and the Main Plots in 1603. James tightened up security in response, and reaffirmed the existing statutes, adding to the severity of the punishments for those who continued to resist conversion. Understandably, perhaps, the Catholics had had enough.

At midnight on 4 November 1605, Guy Fawkes was arrested

while guarding thirty-six barrels of gunpowder in a room near the Palace of Westminster. He intended to set the fuse off when the king and many of his courtiers and members of parliament were to meet there for the state opening of parliament the next day. The conspirators then planned to take control and put James's daughter, the Princess Elizabeth, on the throne. The plot was discovered. The state opening was postponed, and Guy Fawkes was brought before King James I and Secretary of State, Robert Cecil, who interrogated him. Fawkes's defiance provoked James to order he be tortured 'gently' at first, getting to the worst kind by degrees. The torture was carried out in the Tower of London, in a room known today as Guy Fawkes's Room, the only room in England at the time to have a torture machine in it known as a 'rack'. The signature on Fawkes's confession, a mere scrawl, is said to be evidence of the lengths the interrogators went to in their efforts to get him to confess.

It has to be said that the Catholics hadn't behaved in an exemplary manner. After all, the reformation had started as a result of an abuse of power by Catholics – mainly in the blatantly commercial selling of indulgences. They had committed their share of killings on religious grounds and English Catholics had continued to plot against Elizabeth I. However, two wrongs do not make a right.

Within a week, Fawkes's fellow conspirators had been rounded up. They were dragged through the city, hung by the neck, then taken down from the gallows to be disembowelled while still alive, beheaded, then quartered, and their dismembered remains sent to the four corners of the kingdom to be displayed.

Since 1605, 5 November has been celebrated around England as Guy Fawkes Day, with fireworks and a traditional effigy of the man burnt on a bonfire. The custom continues to this day, with the town of Lewes claiming their Bonfire Night Celebrations the biggest in the world.

Explore further

The acts of parliament mentioned above can be found in Tanner's *Tudor Constitutional Documents* (B123). For more information on the Lewes Bonfire Celebrations, visit their website at lewesbonfirecelebrations.com. If you're interested in how the tensions between Catholics and Protestants affected artistic life in this period, I'd recommend Clare Asquith's *Shadowplay* (B5), in which an intriguing theory is put forward about a secret code that Shakespeare used which was used and recognised by recusants – was he one? What do you think?

Bones

St Stephen's Chapel, The Palace of Westminster, London, 20 April 1653—Oliver Cromwell, Lord Protector of the Commonwealth of England, Scotland and Ireland, dismisses the Rump Parliament.

The building in which the English parliament assembled in 1640 was very different from the House of Commons as it is today. Back then, the walls of the long medieval hall in which parliament had met since 1547 were decorated with angels, the ceiling with stars. Peacock feathers had been used to paint the former; down from the breasts of royal swans to paint the latter and squirrels' tails to paint the saints around what used to be the altar. The room had previously been a chapel – first, the chapel of St Stephen's College, then, after the reformation, the chapel of the Palace of Westminster. Henry VIII moved the court to the Palace of Whitehall after a fire in 1512. His son, Edward VI, decreed it should be the permanent meeting place for the House of Commons. In the modern Palace of Westminster, St Stephen's Hall stands over the site of the medieval chapel and is roughly the same size as the original.

Nowadays, we're used to a stable, constitutional monarchy and a parliament which meets for a period of over 40 weeks every year. In the 1600s, things were very different.

Charles I did not have a very constructive relationship with his parliament (to put it mildly) and many of the laws which regulate parliament's structure and sittings today (including the existence of the House of Lords) were instigated as a result of – and developed out of a reactionary move against – Charles I's insistence on his divine rights as sovereign. Differences of opinion degenerated into threatening behaviour with drawn swords on either side. It seemed that where parliamentary debate was unable to exist, there was no alternative to a civil war. Loyalties throughout the land were divided, but not on every count. Nationally, people were loyal to their heritage and were prepared to defend their way of life against forced change; on matters of the soul they would not be imposed upon; but they could not agree on the issue of what was right – right in precedent and principle; right for the kingdom in practice and pragmatism; right for them in profit and pursuit of freedom through a process of reasonable discussion. As a result, both sides drew on what forces and loyalties they could, and the two sides ended up standing on the same soil, on two sides of an ideological borderline, facing each other, prepared to fight to the death. Over a series of battles, Cromwell emerged the victor and the King lost not just the war, but, in 1649, his head.

The balance of power was maintained through a show of force and the silencing of opposing views, leading to quick decisions about religious reform and the redistribution of wealth, but much slower progress on decision-making when it came to coming up with a constitution, with Cromwell and Sir Henry Vane having very different views on what the outcome should be, hotly debating what the nature of the balance of civil and military power should be; who should constitute the parliament; in what form; whether or not to hold elections; and if so, when. Power was at stake. Cromwell was losing patience with parliament – and he had the support of the army.

On 20 April 1653, Cromwell attended parliament, having been warned that Vane was planning to push through a version of the election bill with which Cromwell disagreed. In the event, Cromwell ended up dissolving parliament (a repeat of Charles I's actions earlier that century) in order to avoid the result Vane wanted. And that was the start of the Protectorate.

Plus ça change, plus c'est la même chose. (The more things change, the more they stay the same).

No direct transcript of Cromwell's speech has survived. All we have are ear- and eyewitness accounts which differ in form while sharing a common substance. The words Cromwell speaks in the riddle are taken from a 1767 account by Thomas Salmon:

> [Cromwell] commanded the Speaker to leave the chair, and told [them] that they had sat long enough, unless they had done more good, crying out, You are no longer a Parliament, I say you are no Parliament. He told Sir Henry Vane, that he was a juggler; Henry Martin and Sir Peter Wentworth, that they were whoremasters; Tom Chaloner, that he was a drunkard; and Allen the goldsmith, that he cheated the public. Then he bid one of his soldiers take away that fool's bauble, the mace, and [Thomas] Harrison pulled the Speaker out of the Chair; and Cromwell having turned them all out of the house, locked up the doors, and returned to Whitehall.

An earlier account can be found in Bulstrode Whitelocke's *Memorials*. Dickens seems to have drawn on both sources for his version.

A more florid version appears in Wrangham's 1816 revised edition of Thomas Mortimer's *The British Plutarch*, in which the following note is added:

> The following piece, said to have been found lately among some papers, which formerly belonged to Oliver Cromwell, is supposed to be a copy of the very words addressed by him to the members of the Long Parliament, when he turned them

out of the house. It was communicated to the Annual Register for 1767, by a person, who signed his name, 'T. Ireton,' and said the paper was marked with the following words, 'Spoken by Oliver Cromwell, when he put an end to the Long Parliament:'

> "It is high time for me to put an end to your sitting in this place; which ye have dishonoured by your contempt of all virtue, and defiled by your practice of every vice. Ye are a factious crew, and enemies to all good government. Ye are a pack of mercenary wretches and would, like Esau, sell your country for a mess of pottage; and like Judas, betray your God for a few pieces of money. Is there a single Virtue now remaining among you? Is there one vice ye do not possess? Ye have no more religion than my horse! Gold is your God. Which of you have not bartered away your conscience for bribes? Is there a man among you, that has the least care for the good of the Commonwealth? Ye sordid prostitutes! Have you not defiled this sacred place, and turned the Lord's Temple *into a den of thieves*? By your immoral principles and wicked practices ye are grown intolerably odious to the whole Nation.
>
> Your country, therefore, calls upon me to cleanse this Augean Stable, by putting a final period to your iniquitous proceedings in this house; and which, by God's help, and the strength He hath given me, I am now come to do. I command you, therefore, upon the peril of your lives, to depart immediately out of this Place. Go! Get ye out! Make haste! Ye venal slaves, begone!—So!—Take away that shining bauble there, and lock up the doors."

This is the time of the Conference of Grandees of which Whitelocke gives his full account – a conference in which the discussion ranged as to whether the Commonwealth should be governed as a monarchy or a republic which preceded and probably pre-empted Cromwell's calculated power move of 20 April 1653, which forms the subject of this riddle. Carlyle had a very low opinion of Whitelocke, and his commentary on Whitelocke's account of the conference is well worth reproducing:

> ... our learned Bulstrode's report of this Conference is very dim, very languid: nay Bulstrode, as we have found elsewhere, has a kind of dramaturgic turn in him, indeed an occasional poetic friskiness; most unexpected, as if the hippopotamus should show a tendency to dance; – which painfully deducts from one's confidence in Bulstrode's entire accuracy on such occasions! Here and there the multitudinous Paper Masses of learned Bulstrode do seem to smack a little of the date when he redacted them, – posterior to the Everblessed Restoration, not prior to it. We shall, nevertheless, excerpt this dramaturgic Report of Conference: the reader will be willing to examine, with his own eyes, even as in a glass darkly, any feature of that time; and he can remember always that a learned Bulstrode's fat terrene mind, imaging a heroic Cromwell and his affairs, is a very dark glass indeed!

Explore further

Belloc's version of the events of the period (B12) gives a particularly clear account of the events leading up to the Civil War up to the execution of Charles I which is well worth reading, as is Dickens' version in *A Child's History of England* (B31 – Volume 3, Chapter 34, pp 236–237).

For more information on the old Palace of Westminster, see Walter Thornbury's *Old and New London* (B127) and the articles about the building on the UK Parliament website (C10, C11). The accounts of Cromwell's words when dismissing the Long Parliament can be found in Thomas Salmon's *A New Geographical and Historical Grammar ...* (B110 – p 264), and Wrangham's edition of Mortimer's *British Plutarch* (B80 – pp 287/8). More detailed accounts of the lead-up to Cromwell's dismissal of parliament and its aftermath can be found in John Wade's *British History, Chronologically Arranged* ... (B138) and Bulstrode Whitelocke's *Memorials* (B143), which Carlyle was so disparaging of in his book on Cromwell (B19).

Bonfire

The Old Marketplace (Place du Vieux-Marché), Rouen, France, 1431—Joan of Arc (c. *1412–31) is burnt at the stake, having been convicted of being a lapsed heretic.*

In this riddle, the so-called Hundred Years' War between the kingdoms of England and France has been raging on and off for 94 years. It is to last another 22 (116 years in total, from 1337 to 1453). In 1431, when this event takes place, Rouen is in the possession of the English – as are the rest of Normandy, Brittany, Gascony, Paris and much of Champagne. The Burgundians are squabbling with the Armagnacs. War stretches over the country like a pall, allowing the English to take advantage of the situation and gain more land.

They would probably have taken over even more had it not been for a 17-year-old girl we now know as Joan of Arc. She was a child of her age, born to meet the needs of her country – as Shakespeare, Churchill, Martin Luther King or Gandhi did in their days.

She was born Jehanne Darc. Her story is well documented, in a range of primary sources. She came into her own one summer's day, when she was 13. She was in her father's garden in the small village of Domrémy when she heard a mysterious voice. She was neither the first to do so, nor the last. Before her came Moses and Socrates; after her came Gandhi and Dickens, all of whom admitted to hearing voices. Jehanne believed the voice she heard was the voice of God – not a particularly safe admission at a time when people were accused of the crimes of witchcraft and sorcery, crimes which typically lead to a violent and painful death.

At 16, she was told to go to a certain nobleman of the court (Captain Robert de Baudricourt) at Vaucouleurs and get him to arrange an audience for her with the Dauphin (the word literally means dolphin and alludes to a nickname which developed into a hereditary title and passed to the French crown in 1349, when the Dauphiné territory which was previously independent was bought by King Philip VI of France and the condition that the title of Dauphin was given to the heir to the throne was part of the deal). At first, the captain didn't take her seriously, but when she announced that the French had lost the Battle of the Herrings, and it turned out to be true, he gave her the benefit of the doubt and escorted her safely through occupied territory and into the Dauphin's presence at Chinon.

Mistrusting her motives, the courtiers decided they would have one of their number swap places with the Dauphin to receive her, but she knew exactly who the real Dauphin was and told him that God had told her that she was the only person who could save France – a proposition which is hard to prove or disprove except in the act. She even told the Dauphin things he said he'd only ever revealed to God in prayer. Nevertheless, they did what they could to probe her character, her reputation, her sanity and her state of mind. After three weeks, the panel advised the Dauphin that she seemed genuine; that he would lose nothing if he listened to her; and that if he didn't, he risked ignoring a true messenger of God, sent to help them in their hour of need – for the war wasn't going in favour of the French. It says something about this country girl, who was able to rebut her interrogators in a way that must have been reminiscent of Jesus, as a child, disputing the finer points of scripture and the law with the elders in the temple.

Her skill was in battle strategy. Finding it safer and easier to dress as a man, she led the French troops to victory, breaking the Siege of Orléans, regaining Troyes, winning the Battle of Patay, and gaining a real and symbolic victory for France by bringing

Reims back under French rule, allowing the Dauphin to be crowned King Charles VII of France in the French equivalent of Westminster Abbey – Reims being the site of royal coronations from 752 until the demise of the French monarchy. This was an important move politically since, in 1422, King Charles VI of France had passed the French crown on to his son-in-law Henry V of England and his heirs in the Treaty of Troyes, cutting off his son the Dauphin Charles from the possibility of succeeding to the throne (this was the same Charles whom Jean helped crown). Charles VI of France's act was contrary to the French laws of succession, which stated that the French crown couldn't just be handed over like this. Until the kings of France could sort it out, there was a dual monarchy that lasted until 1453 when the resolution they came to finally helped end the 'Hundred Years' War'.

Joan of Arc had been instructed by her divine guide to advise the king to press on immediately with further battles, but he leaned towards a negotiated peace settlement. This led to the Maid of Orléans (as Joan of Arc is also known) being captured by the French and sold to the English at Compiègne, to be tried on charges of heresy and witchcraft by her own countrymen acting on behalf of their English overlords.

Her interrogation was lengthy. Her trial sessions, which are fully documented, were convoluted. At the end of the tiring process, she admitted to heresy and was absolved, yet still kept in prison. When she took back her statement, she gave the prosecutors what they were looking for – grounds to execute her for being a lapsed heretic. You see, it was somewhat difficult to prove that someone was a heretic, but if they admitted it, and resolved not to behave the way they had, but then went back to their old ways, it was proof they were consciously choosing to behave in a manner they had fully admitted in court was contrary to accepted doctrine. How they got people to leap through these hoops, of course, was somewhat murky – inquisitors were particularly good at producing these sequences of events.

Joan of Arc was burned at the stake on 30 May 1431. Her entrails were removed and burned to ash. Her bones were burned separately. The remains of both were thrown into the Seine to prevent people from gathering any relics from the site.

After 21 years, Jehanne's mother, Isabelle de Lys (born Romée – the family was ennobled in 1429 and the name 'de Lys' was registered to them in 1430) petitioned the Pope, in tears, to retry the case posthumously as she believed her daughter innocent and wrongfully executed. Witnesses came forth to testify in Jehanne's favour, and the court ruled that Jehanne had been unjustly convicted and reversed the ruling on a technicality.

Her white banner inspired the inclusion of the central white band in the *tricolore* French flag after the 1789 revolution; and in 1849, the Bishop of Orléans led a fervent campaign to get her canonised. She was made a saint in 1920.

She wasn't everyone's idea of a heroine. Both Shakespeare and Voltaire characterised her unfavourably. And in his play, *Gilles and Jeanne*, Georg Kaiser explores the links between Joan of Arc and a notorious criminal of the time, Gilles de Rais.

She has inspired numerous artistic and cultural works, and her name has been associated with other young heroines who fought for their countries and met similar ends, such as Manto Mavrogenous (1796–1840) and Laskarina Bouboulina (1771–1825), heroines of the Greek War of Independence; Emilia Plater (1806–31), who fought for Poland's independence from Russia in the Polish-Russian War of 1831, along with several other women; 22-year-old Lakshmibai, the Rani of Jhansi (1828–58), who defended the state of Jhansi which she ruled over against the English; Chinese liberal reformist Sieh King King (1886–?); Yanitza Martinay (*c.* 1890–?), heroine of the Albanian War of Independence; and Korean independence fighter Gwan-sun Ryu (1904–20).

Explore further

A complete translation of the primary sources for Joan of Arc's trial can be found in WP Barrett's *The Trial of Jeanne D'Arc* (B11). There's also a good bibliography on the Jeanne d'arc la pucelle website (C40), where you can also find a depiction of her coat of arms (C52).

A list of witches, witch trials and killings in France from the sixth century onwards can be found on Marc Carlson's University of Tulsa website (C18). A worldwide list can be found on the Sacred Texts website (C14). Both lists extend well into the twentieth century. And if you think anything changed in the twenty-first, think again. In 2012, two people were jailed in the UK for murdering a teenage relative they believed was practising witchcraft. According to an article in *The Guardian* published in March that year, between 2002 and 2012, Scotland Yard looked into 83 cases of abuse associated with ritualistic beliefs, such as witchcraft, and brought 17 of these cases to trial (A36).

And if you happen to hear voices, you're not alone (no pun intended). There's a whole bunch of people with varying claims to fame who are celebrated at *Intervoice,* The International Hearing Voices Network (C82). You can visit the organization's website at intervoiceonline.org.

Cinders

A cottage on the Isle of Athelney, 878 CE—King Alfred, driven back by the invading Danish army, hiding out incognito, lets his hostess's loaves burn as he contemplates his options.

The man in the story is King Alfred, King of Wessex, then King of the Anglo-Saxons. The story which forms the basis of this riddle, more commonly known as 'King Alfred burns the cakes', is first recounted in the twelfth century by St Neot (or Neots), but is later interpolated in a sixteenth century version of Asser's ninth century account of Alfred's life.

Neot's version describes the king staying for a while in the house of a shepherd (or neatherd in some translations) with both him and his wife present. I have taken the liberty of embroidering the dynamics somewhat. The emphasis on differing religious beliefs is taken directly from Neot's account.

The scene marks an important turning point in the tide of British history. Prior to ending up in this cottage, the Vikings ruled over most of Britain, with the exception of Wessex. In 876, after a series of battles, King Alfred, having gained the upper hand and negotiated a peace treaty with the Danes, spent Christmas in Chippenham. The Danes broke the treaty, attacked the town and killed most of its inhabitants. The king managed to flee to the marshes of Somerset with a small band of followers where he decided to camp out, and from there stage his counter-attacks. It is between his flight and his counter-attacks that this scene presumably must have occurred. By 878, King Alfred had managed to successfully demonstrate superiority, negotiate a stable treaty – the *Treaty of Alfred and Guthrum* – which instituted the Danelaw and allowed peaceful coexistence between the Danes and the Saxons.

Recent research by Professor Rory McTurk, a specialist in Norse literature, has revealed an earlier literary source for the 'cakes' story. It features in a Norse saga in relation to Ragnar Hairybreeks. Professor McTurk argues that the Ragnar story may well have circulated in oral form, with a political propaganda slant aimed at showing King Alfred in a less than ideal light: tired, worn out, lacking concentration and, using dough as a metaphor – in an suitably embellished version by a gifted story-teller – lacking the power to rise to the occasion in more senses than one.

Other stories about King Alfred and his times have come down to us in written form, yet have the sense of being spun out of an oral tradition. One of these features in both Asser's *Life* and *The Annals of St Neots*. It tells of an ominous magical banner which the Danes held in extremely high regard and which they flew at the head of their fleet. It featured a black raven, woven by Ragnar's sisters in less than a day, and invested with witchcraft. It was said that it would flap its wings if the Danish forces were to win the battle they were about to fight, and be still if they were to be defeated. The Anglo-Saxon chronicle (started by King Alfred) states that the banner was captured by the English in 878.

The story of a magical black raven banner leading troops into battle and predicting the outcome is repeated in the tales of the Norse Jarls of Orkney of the Battle of Clontarf (1014). Other banners feature in the Norse Heimskringla saga, in accounts of the Battle of Stamford Bridge and of the Battle of Hastings (1066).

The story of how King Alfred learned to read forms part of Asser's *Life*. It's a story that has been repeated in many popular accounts of King Alfred the Great's life since then. However, what most of these accounts fail to recognise is that Asser states that Alfred learned to read when he was 13, and that prior to that, he 'listened with serious attention to the Saxon poems which he often heard recited, and easily retained them in his docile memory'.

Alfred only learned to read because his stepmother showed him and his brothers a beautifully illuminated book and promised to give it to whichever one of them could show they could read it first. Alfred became obsessed with the wonder of the written word and successfully completed the challenge. Asser states that

> ... he could not gratify his most ardent wish to learn the liberal arts, because, as he said, there were no good readers at that time in all the kingdom of the West-Saxons.
>
> This he confessed, with many lamentations and sighs, to have been one of his greatest difficulties and impediments in this life, namely, that when he was young and had the capacity for learning, he could not find teachers; but, when he was more advanced in life, he was harassed by so many diseases

> unknown to all the physicians of this island, as well as by internal and external anxieties of sovereignty, and by continual invasions of the pagans, and had his teachers and writers also so much disturbed, that there was no time for reading. But yet among the impediments of this present life, from infancy up to the present time, and, as I believe, even until his death, he continued to feel the same insatiable desire of knowledge, and still aspires after it.

Although Asser asserts that Alfred was taught to read at 13 by his mother, his mother had died when he was seven. His father subsequently married Charlemagne's great-granddaughter, Judith, who at the time was twelve years old, making her 18 at the time the story is supposed to have taken place.

King Alfred kept a commonplace book, the use of which is described in Asser's *Life*, and made sure his children were brought up being taught the liberal arts, including the art of reading, but also made sure they learned Saxon poetry by heart.

Another story, which is alluded to in this Treasure Trove riddle, is that of King Alfred repeatedly entering the Danish camp disguised as a minstrel in order to find out what the Danes' battle strategy and war plans were. Foxe cites prior sources for this tale, stating that King Alfred would have sung in Saxon. What these chroniclers don't explain is why his doing so would have appealed to the Danes.

I've left this as a riddle within a riddle for readers to engage with.

King Alfred was largely responsible for the further establishment of Christianity throughout England, for establishing a network of fortified *burhs*, which acted as well-connected centres of trade and defence, for building up the English navy, for instituting centres of learning across his domains, for translating many works into the vernacular and distributing them across these centres of learning, for effectively setting the foundations for English culture and for reforming the legal system. It is for this unique mix of learning, piety, diplomacy, policy and battle strategy that he has, since the sixteenth century, been considered 'Alfred the Great'.

Explore further

Readable accounts of King Alfred's life can be found in Barbara Yorke's article for *History Today* which poses the question *Alfred the Great: The Most Perfect Man in History?* (A52) and Justin Pollard's book, *Alfred the Great* (B94). You might, however, want to balance your reading of the latter by also taking in Daniel Hannan's review of it in *The Telegraph*, which, incidentally, starts off by quoting Pollard's view that 'If Alfred is remembered at all today, it is for the legend of burning the cakes' (A19).

If you want to go further, why not start by taking a look at early sources in translation? They're accessible and enlightening. Both Asser's *Life of King Alfred* and St Neot's *Annals* are available on line in Stevenson's edition (B118). The former is available in Cook's edition (B26). Further information about St Neot's account can be found in an article by Malcolm Godden in the scholarly journal, *Anglo-Saxon England* (A16). A later elaboration of the 'cakes' story can be found in the 1570 edition of Foxe's *Actes and Monuments* (usually referred to as *Foxe's Book of Martyrs*), (C30 – Book 3, p 201), which has Alfred staying in the cottage of an illiterate swineherd called Dunwolfus, educating him in return for his hospitality, after which he is made Bishop of Winchester.

Elephants

A plateau in the Franco-Italian Alps, 218 BCE—The Carthaginian general, Hannibal Barca, rests during his crossing of the Alps during his campaign to attack Rome via an overland route.

Hannibal Barca was from Carthage, the capital of the Carthaginian Empire which was founded by the Phoenician Queen Dido, who features in Virgil's *Aeneid*. Abandoned by the lover she has sheltered, who leaves her and subsequently founds Rome, she dies with a curse on her lips, "Rise up from my bones, avenging spirit" (B135 – Book 4, Lines 612–29). That spirit, later writers saw realised in the figure of Hannibal.

The enduring fascination with Hannibal arguably lies in his intriguing character and tactical ability, the particularly dramatic circumstances of his life, and the sheer daring of his campaigns and their unprecedented scale for their time. As Livy states,

> No states, no nations ever met in arms greater in strength or richer in resources; these Powers themselves had never before been in so high a state of efficiency or better prepared to stand the strain of a long war; they were no strangers to each other's tactics.
> (B64 – Book 21, Chapter 1, Section 2 – Volume 5, pp 2–3).

Rome and Carthage were the two main powers in the Mediterranean in the third century BCE. They first locked horns over Sicily. Carthage had the advantage at sea; Rome had the advantage on land. It took over 100 years and the loss of hundreds of thousands of lives in battle, but the Romans finally won. The series of wars they fought to emerge victorious are called the Punic Wars – the adjective is derived from the Carthaginians' Phoenician heritage.

In Silius Italicus' account, the Carthaginians elect to sacrifice Hannibal's firstborn son to the gods. Italicus states this was a political move – possibly by Hanno II the Great, an ardent anti-war campaigner – to weaken Hannibal's resolve to pursue the invasion of Italy. In a dramatic shift of events, Hannibal's wife, Imilce, stands up to them so ferociously, they allow Hannibal to choose, for himself, whether to obey or defy the gods, a turn of events which impels Hannibal in exactly the opposite direction to that which Hanno may have intended, choosing to sacrifice the sons of thousands of Roman mothers rather than his own son, who, he argued, should live to follow in his footsteps and continue to expand and add to the Carthaginian empire. And so it was that Hannibal started his campaign.

The speech Hannibal gives in the riddle is based loosely on the speech invented by Livy in his *History of Rome* (B64 – Book 21, Chapter 21, Section 30 – Volume 5, pp 86/7).

When Napoleon crossed the Alps, he reputedly carved his name on a rock, near an inscription Hannibal had made. The inscriptions are depicted in Jacques-Louis David's portrait of *Napoleon Crossing the Alps*, but, as both generals are likely to have taken different routes, the story is probably just a pictorial allegory linking Napoleon with Hannibal.

After his victories in the battles of Trebia, Trasimene and Cannae, fought on Italian soil, Hannibal returned to Carthage to defend his native land against a counter-invasion by Roman forces, led by the Roman general Scipio, in whom Hannibal met his match. Defeated at the battle of Zama, Hannibal met Scipio later at Ephesus. The meeting offered an opportunity for both to reflect on their careers. The conversation turned to historic generals, with Hannibal ranking Alexander the Great first, then Pyrrhus of Epirus (of Pyrrhic victory fame), then himself. "And if you had not been defeated by me?" asked Scipio, quietly. "Then myself, first of all," granted Hannibal, in an oblique acknowledgement of Scipio's ultimate victory over him.

Explore further

The main classical sources that cover Hannibal's campaign are Livy's *History of Rome* (B64) and *Periochae* (C46); Polybius' *Histories* (B97 – Book 9, Chapters 22–26) and Appian's *Roman History* (B3 – Book 7 – Volume 1, pp 303–399). Others include works by Cornelius Nepos (B85); Silius Italicus (B52); Plutarch (B93 – *Lucullus* – Volume 2, pp 572–575, *Fabius Maximus* – Volume 3, pp 118–197, *Titus Flaminius* – Volume 10, pp 322–387 and *Marcellus* – Volume 5, pp 436–523); and Cassius Dio (B25 – Books

13–17, 19; pp 54–275, 300–331 respectively).

One of the most enduring questions about Hannibal's tactics is the question of how he got his elephants to Iberia, and on to Gaul, through Gaul, over the Alps and on into Italy. They didn't all make it. How did he feed them? What was the precise route the army took? We still don't have all the answers, and evidence from numismatics (A34) and geoarchaeology (C37) is informing some of the recent attempts to answer these questions.

The connections between Hannibal and Napoleon are worth looking at, as are the depictions of those connections by artists such as David (C24) and Delaroche (C26). Why not take a look at the 1929 article by John Spaeth in *The Classical Journal* to explore this theme further (A44)?

In modern times, Hannibal has fascinated authors such as Andreas Kluth, who wrote *Hannibal and Me: What History's Greatest Strategist Can Teach Us About Success and Failure* (B59, C41). What might *you* find that fascinates you about Hannibal, and how might *you* tell his story?

G

1440s—Johannes Gutenberg invents moveable type.

The protagonist in this scene is a single, small piece of moveable type – a letter 'G' – in Johannes Gutenberg's workshop. It's the hand-carved master for a single letter, from which a cast is made and a number of copies are taken. You'd think that this would have been easy enough to do – there are only twenty-six letters, after all. No. Gutenberg was such a perfectionist, he cast several versions of each letter, in various widths, so that each line of text he put together looked as it had been laid out perfectly. And don't forget punctuation marks and spaces – lots of different widths of spaces. And, of course, each letter comes in two versions – upper and lower case.

Gutenberg didn't invent moveable type – it had been used in eleventh century China and there was a precedent in Europe for printing books, illustrations and pamphlets using carved wooden or metal blocks. Gutenberg's invention allowed for a much quicker printing process, though, once the type had been created.

For Gutenberg, each piece of type had to be designed, taking into account how the letters would fit next to each other; how much space to leave between them; how much space to leave between lines; where the letter should be placed on each piece of type; how all the pieces would fit together on the composing stick; and how they would be secured in the *forme* (the technical term for the frame which holds the type for a single page in place). He'd check each hand-carved piece for accuracy. This was done by taking a print by putting it in a candle flame, thus covering it with soot, and making a test print called a 'smoke proof'. After any minor adjustments were made, each piece was hardened – usually in fire, but sometimes using cyanide or other carbon-rich materials to increase the hardness of the outer surface of the metal. From the heat of the fire, each piece would be plunged into cold water to get the metal to contract quickly. Then a mould would be made of each piece from softer metal and a molten alloy of lead, tin and antimony poured in. This hardened very quickly, allowing multiple copies to be made from the same mould reasonably fast, although it was a labour-intensive process.

Gutenberg started off printing single-page items such as poems in German, or indulgences for the Catholic Church. The work he's most famous for, however, is the Gutenberg Bible, of which around a hundred and eighty copies were printed, some on vellum. It's thought that only twenty-one complete copies are known to be in existence today. The technology Gutenberg invented sparked an intellectual revolution. Europe went from having hardly any printed books in 1440 to having around thirty thousand titles by 1500. It was an invention that literally changed the world.

Explore further

Each piece of moveable type has clearly defined parts. The copies of the original letters are arranged on a composing stick and placed in a *forme*, from which a print is taken. You can find out more about the terminology in an annotated diagram on Wikimedia (C38 – in context at C83).

There has been speculation about Laurence Koster's role in the development of moveable type in Europe. The story goes that he made a set of letters from bark for his grandchildren, then extended the idea of using wooden letters as moveable type from there. The full story can be found alongside a critique of certain parts of it in the entry for *Printing* in 1842 edition of the Encyclopedia Britannica (A9).

For more information on the development of printing in China, see Joseph Needham's *The Shorter Science and Civilisation in China* (B84 – Volume 4, pp 14 ff), although it was much more widely used in Korea at the time. The earliest extant copy of a book printed in moveable type is the Korean *Jikji simgyeong (The Anthology of Great Buddhist Priests' Zen Teachings)* of 1377. References exist to books produced in this manner in Korea before this one, but this is the earliest known copy still in existence.

Some artists and designers today still find inspiration in letterpress forms and moveable type. You might want to explore the work of Alan Kitching (thetypographyworkshop.com) – or the artists whose work is featured in Cathie Saunders and Martha Chiplis' book, *For the Love of Letterpress* (B112).

Hoopoe

The court of King Solomon The Wise, c. *950 BCE—The arrival of the Queen of Sheba.*

Renowned for their wisdom, the meeting of King Solomon and the Queen of Sheba was seen to be significant enough to warrant its inclusion in the Bible (1 Kings, 10:1–13; 2 Chronicles, 9:1–12), the Qur'an (Surahs 27, 34) and the Ethiopian *Kebra Negast*. Arguably the most interesting account, though, comes from the Abyssinian version of the tale. When the meeting happened is unclear. The accepted dates for King Solomon's reign are between 970 and 931 BCE, with the conjectured date of 950 BCE cited here solely because it is a round number that lies roughly in the middle of the range.

King Solomon was the first ruler of the united kingdoms of Israel and Judah. On ascending the throne, rather than asking God for riches or a long life, he asked that he might be given wisdom to rule with understanding, with discrimination and knowledge of good and evil to allow him to judge fairly. God, pleased with his request, granted him wisdom, riches and honour, on condition that he keep his commandments.

He is believed to have written three of the books of the Old Testament: The Book of Proverbs, Ecclesiastes, and the Song of Songs. He was the son of King David, author of the Book of Psalms. Solomon's mechanical throne was designed to strike awe and fear in his petitioners like the two mothers who disputed their relation to a child, for instance (1 Kings, 3:16–28). His wealth was immense and the exchange of gifts between the two rulers was accordingly lavish, but it was for the exchange of wisdom that the Queen is said to have travelled from Ethiopia to Jerusalem to meet the king Solomon. His answers to the questions featured in this Treasure Trove riddle were:

1. What is evil?
   The eyes of the Lord in every place monitor good and evil, and in them is the definition.
2. Are the eyes or the ears superior?
   The hearing ear and the seeing eye, the Lord hath made both.
   Degrees of deafness and blindness, these are man's province, and measurable.

3. What is the most powerful organ of the body?
   Death and life are in the power of the tongue.
4. How are body and spirit connected?
   The baseness of spirits is derived from their bodies.
   The nobility of bodies is derived from their spirits.

Further riddles feature in Jewish texts and commentaries on books of the Bible.

For all his wisdom, according to the account in 1 Kings 11:1–12, Solomon built temples for his wives to worship their own gods, but having been warned against doing so three times by the God of Israel, was eventually punished by Him – the punishment causing a rift between the Kingdom of Judah and the Kingdom of Israel after his death.

According to the *Kebra Negast*, King Solomon and Bilkis – as her name appears in that work – have a child, who ends up stealing the Ark of the Covenant from Jerusalem (leaving another Ark there) and taking it to Ethiopia where it is claimed it is preserved to this day. The wise rulers' relationship is assumed by Rudyard Kipling in his story of *The Butterfly that Stamped* in *The Just So Stories*. In this story, as in the accounts of Solomon's powers in the *Kebra Negast* and in the Qur'an (34:12), King Solomon is depicted as having the power to control djinns. The earliest known literary source which describes this aspect of his powers is the Gnostic text known as *The Apocalypse of Adam* and is also mentioned in the *Testament of Solomon*, thought to date from around the first century CE.

Explore further

The Abyssinian account of the story which inspired this riddle can be found in an English translation by the Princeton scholar, Dr Enno Littman (B63). I am indebted to Lady Jewel for the questions within the riddle, which feature in her book *Keeper of the Ark* (B56 – pp 146–148).

You'll find more Solomonic riddles and further information about King Solomon's throne in Louis Ginzberg's *The Legends of the Jews* (B38 – Vol 4, pp 145–149 and 157–160) and you can explore riddles further in Jacques Issaverdens' *The Uncanonical Writings of the Old Testament* (B51 – pp 211–215), and Solomon Schechter's article on *The Riddles of Solomon* in *Folk-Lore* (A40). To explore the wide and varying significance and use of riddles in different cultures, the collection of essays edited by Galit Hasan-Rokem and David Shulman entitled *Untying the Knot* is well worth a peek (B43).

To explore the stories of Solomon and Bilkis in Islam further, two potential launching pads are Jamal Elias's paper, *Prophecy, Power and Propriety: The Encounter of Solomon and the Queen of Sheba* (A12) which gives an introduction to their reception in the Arabian tradition and a masterful essay by another Princeton scholar, Prof Michael Barry, in which he covers the story from the Persian perspective and outlines the way in which legends of King Solomon from the Jewish tradition merged with mythical stories of King Jamshêd to create a powerful symbol – at once culturally specific and universally relevant (A4). Incidentally, 'Attâr's *Canticle of the Birds* (the essay appears in a sumptuous edition of this work) and the *Koran* both provide clues as to why this riddle is entitled 'Hoopoe'. In 'Attâr's work, the Hoopoe acts as guide to a flock of birds, and symbolises a journey towards enlightenment – in this case, depicted as a metaphorical Sufic journey, the goal of which, in the metaphor, is to reach the mythical phoenix-like bird, the Simurgh. When they do, they find … well, I'll leave you to find that out for yourself.

The texts referred to above in which Solomon's power over djinns is described can be found in the *Targum Sheni to the Book of Esther* (B39), in George W MacRae's translation of *The Apocalypse of Adam* (C48), and in Chester McCown's commentary to his edition of *The Testament of Solomon* (B75 – pp 43 ff).

If you feel a bit of Indiana Jones fever coming on, the question of where the Ark of the Covenant is now is still open. Journalists Paul Raffaele (A37) and Hillel Fendel (C29) write tantalisingly of its existence… but if the *Kebra Negast* is to be believed, and there were two Arks, which might this one be, and where might the other be?

KKM

The Giza Plateau, c. *2540 BCE—The construction of the pyramid of Menkaure, the third and last of the great pyramids of Giza.*

This riddle's title is derived from the initials of the names of the three Old Kingdom pharaohs of the Fourth Dynasty whose pyramids dominate the Giza plateau – Khufu, Khafra and Menkaure. The river is the Nile and the constellation of Orion is a reference to the controversial theory put forward by Robert Bauval that the positions of the Great Pyramids of Giza match those of the stars in Orion's belt. We are witnessing the construction of the third pyramid, that of Menkaure (sometimes also referred to as Mycerinus).

Herodotus describes Menkaure as a munificent, liberal ruler, compensating people for miscarriages of justice from his own purse, and a ruler who 'gave liberty to the people … to return to their own business and to their sacrifices'. Earlier pyramid projects, such as Snefru's Red Pyramid at Dahshur, may well have been completed by prisoners of war, judging by official inscriptions such as those on the Palermo Stone. Recently, archaeologists have argued that the Giza pyramids were not built by slave labour, but by skilled workers, with a possible element of conscription.

The first pyramid in Egypt – a step pyramid – was built by Zoser *c.* 3000 BCE. The first smooth-sided pyramid in Egypt was built in *c.* 2950 BCE during the reign of Snefru. The so-called Bent Pyramid in the same complex, at Dahshur, shows a transition between the earlier style of building, in which stones were laid at an angle to the ground, to the more stable method of placing them parallel to the ground.

Herodotus claims that 100,000 men worked to build the Great Pyramid at a time, with workers rotating in 3-month cycles.

Herodotus also states that when an oracle foretold that Menkaure should only live for 6 more years, he remonstrated with the priests, arguing that he had reopened their gods' temples and caused more prosperity than his forbears. The response was that by doing so, he had interfered with a previous prophecy that Egypt should endure 150 years of misfortune, so his own life had been curtailed. To circumvent the oracle, Menkaure took to partying both day and night, turning night to day with the power of artificial light, thus seeking to live for 12 years, rather than 6, in defiance of the prediction.

The precise date of Menkaure's death isn't known, but he's thought to have reigned between 2530 BCE and 2512 BCE. We know that he died before the pyramid was completed, and that it – and the mortuary temple beside it – were completed by his son, Shepseskaf. The temple complex was excavated and documented in detail by the American archaeologist, George Reisner.

The pyramids of Giza were explored by Colonel Vyse, an English army officer, in 1837, who used gunpowder to blast his way into the monuments. He discovered Menkaure's sarcophagus, arranged for it to be transported to Great Britain on a ship called the *Beatrice*, which sank in the Mediterranean in 1838. Part of Menkaure's wooden coffin, however, was sent over to Britain separately and can be seen at the British Museum.

Explore further

Herodotus' account of Menkaure's life can be found in his *Histories* (B46 – Book 2, Chapters 129–133). As to the question of who built the pyramids, Herodotus' account is in Book 2, Chapter 124 of the *Histories*. See also Sir Ernest Wallis Budge's *The Literature of the Ancient Egyptians* (B16 – p 100) and the articles about Mark Lehner's and Zahi Hawass's excavations at the pyramid (A43, C31 and C34).

Various theories have been advanced as to how the pyramids were built. You can read a short account of Reisner's views in a 1929 article in *Cosmopolitan Magazine* (A38) or his book on Menkaure published in 1931 (B105). An overview of some of the more recent theories can be found on Burke Thomas's website (C76). See also the chapter by Mark Lehner on *Building an Old Kingdom Pyramid* in Zahi Hawass's book *Pyramids: Treasures, Mysteries, and New Discoveries in Egypt* (A29).

Menkaure's sarcophagus is illustrated in the book by Colonel Vyse about his findings at Giza (B137 – Vol 2, p 85). The accession number for the part of Menkaure's coffin in the collection of the British Museum is BM E6647.

Life and Death

A courtroom in the Palace of Justice, Pretoria, 20 April 1964—Defendant Nelson Mandela addresses the court during the Rivonia Trial.

This riddle is based on the speech Nelson Mandela gave during the Rivonia Trial – a court case which was a major landmark in twentieth century history. In 2007, the Rivonia Trial records were included in the UNESCO Memory of the World International Register of documentary heritage.

The words used in the riddle are inspired by the words he used in the speech which survive in audio and written transcription formats. The description of the courtroom is based on pictures from the fiftieth anniversary event held at the Palace of Justice in 2013.

The trial marked a key point in the history of the fight against injustice.

This particular phase of the fight, as it pertained to South Africa, can be said to have started with the formation of the Union of South Africa in 1910, which marginalised the majority black population in favour of the rights of the minority

Afrikaans- and English-speaking white population. There gradually followed the formation of various protest groups, such as the African National Congress (ANC), which arranged a series of civil actions, including non-violent protests, squatters' movements, bus boycotts, civil disobedience campaigns, protest marches and strike actions both independently and jointly with other groups, such as the Communist Party of South Africa (CPSA). Mandela became national president of the ANC Youth League in 1950/1, and as volunteer-in-chief, played a leading role in the Defiance Campaign of 1952, following which the government issued him with the first of several bans from appearing in public. This did not stop Mandela from becoming Deputy President of the ANC in 1952.

In 1955, the ANC along with other anti-apartheid groups jointly adopted 'The Freedom Charter'. This sparked further protests against discriminatory government policy, which were considered to be acts of treason by the government, which sought legal action against the perpetrators.

Among the final 30 of the initial group of 156 people charged with treason in what has since become known as 'The Treason Trial' was Nelson Mandela. The trial lasted 4 years, at the end of which all the defendants were acquitted.

In 1960, police used violence against protesters in Sharpeville. Whether they were provoked or not is unclear, although the number of deaths and eyewitnesses' reports of the lack of warning shots from the police would indicate that, either way, the scale and manner of the police response was such as to cause rightful indignation both nationally and internationally.

It was following this turn of events, and after his release at the end of the Treason Trial, in what could now be called a switch 'from Martin to Malcolm' (from Martin Luther King to Malcom X, that is) that Mandela's thoughts turned from non-violence to violence as a means of protest. Choosing the latter, he ended up as one of the leaders of the military wing of the ANC: Umkhonto

We Sizwe.

Mandela was arrested in 1962, the same year in which the United Nations officially condemned apartheid. The other people involved in this part of the ANC were arrested at their base in Rivonia in 1963, and tried together for plotting against the state.

The trial attracted the attention of the international media and offered Mandela a platform to outline his political views and a reasoned argument for the actions of the ANC towards apartheid to a worldwide audience.

Mandela was sentenced to life imprisonment, rather than death. The decision sparked a number of international sanctions and boycotts against South Africa. Mandela was eventually released in 1990, after 26 years in prison, on the order of the then newly-elected president of South Africa, FW de Klerk.

Following multi-party negotiations to end the rule of apartheid in South Africa, in which Mandela was involved, he was elected president of South Africa following an often violent four-year process of change that culminated in the country's first general election open to all South African nationals. His autobiography, *A Long Road to Freedom* (London: Little, Brown and Company, 1994) was adapted for the screen by William Nicholson and released as a feature film with Idris Elba as Mandela in 2013. Mandela's death coincided with the film's London premiere.

Mandela's name has been applied to a 'Mandelarium' of things which include, as one of clues to this riddle indicates, a species of woodpecker that lived around 3–5 million years ago to a nuclear particle, and a species of spider discovered in 2002, a species of fungus gnat discovered in 2012, a genus of sea slugs, as well as countless public and private spaces. However, many questions surround the life and work of one of the key figures of twentieth century political history.

For many, Mandela was an enlightened leader who was a

figurehead in the fight against apartheid. For others, he was a terrorist who sought to overthrow a legally appointed government through violent means. One of the formulations for the case against Mandela can be found, outlined by the prosecuting attorney in the Rivonia Trial, Percy Yutar, in *Rivonia Unmasked*. His chequered personal life has seen him accused of both adultery and physical abuse.

Furthermore, although the resolution passed, in 1986, Reagan considered it advisable to veto the US Congress's non-binding resolution to (a) recognise the ANC and (b) to call for Mandela's release. Even after Mandela was freed, and elected president, he continued to be included in the US Government's terrorism watch list. His name was only removed when President Bush signed a bill authorising this in 2008, a little less than a decade after Mandela had stepped down from the presidency.

Against the background of Mandela's life, however, on balance, it is more important to ask questions such as:

- Is it the duty of citizens to oppose an unjust law?
- Are you a Malcolm or a Martin? Where would you draw the line in cases such as the choice between violent and non-violent resistance?
- Where such a line is drawn, when – if ever – is it acceptable to cross it?
- What does it take for someone to stand up and be willing to *lay down their life* for a cause?
- To what extent is the decision based on the principle of injustice and to what extent is it subject-related? (Political oppression versus environmental desecration, for instance: both destroy – rather than promote – harmony, and thus are unjust. Do both warrant equal attitudes in terms of resistance?)
- What would it take for you to decide to *lay down your life* in the cause of justice?

Explore further

You can hear the recording of Mandela delivering his speech on the British Library's website (C58). The transcript is available on the Nelson Mandela Centre of Memory website (C51). Information about the documents relating to the Rivonia Trial can be found on the UNESCO website (C21). The photograph on which the description of this riddle is based can be found in the coverage of the fiftieth anniversary of the Rivonia Trial on Jacaranda FM's website (C54). Resolution 1761 requesting member states impose sanctions on South Africa in the aftermath of the trial can be found at the United Nations General Assembly website (C80). The opposition's view is outlined in Lauritz Strydom's *Rivonia Unmasked* (B120).

Dates for events in Mandela's life vary from source to source. For instance, Tom Lodge gives September 1950 as the date Mandela became president of the ANC Youth League in his book on Mandela (B66 – p 254), while the date given in Mandela's *Conversations with Myself* and on the Nelson Mandela Centre of Memory website is 1951 (B72 – p 330, C77).

For more information on the background to the Treason Trial, see *The Freedom Charter* (C72), Mandela's *Freedom in our Lifetime* (C50) on the ANC website and his *We Defy* speech (A32). The trial papers are housed at the University of the Witwatersrand with scans available on line on the university's website (C62).

Information on the Sharpeville Massacre can be found on the South African History Online (SAHO) website (C9).

You can browse through a searchable list of the tributes accorded to Mandela, and the things named after him on the Nelson Mandela Centre of Memory website (C79).

Finally, for an in-depth discussion of the issue of justice and resistance to unjust rule of law, see Thoreau's essay on *Resistance to Civil Government* (A48), John Rawls' book, *A Theory of Justice* (B103), and Stephen Grant's article, *Should We Ever Disobey the Law?* (A17).

Maps

Córdoba, 1492—Christopher Columbus petitions King Ferdinand and Queen Isabella to fund an expedition to seek a western trade route to India.

The scene takes place in the audience room of the Moorish Alcázar castle in Córdoba. The word Alcázar comes from the Arabic *al kasr* (the castle). The man is Christopher Columbus, a Genoese entrepreneur and explorer. The king and queen are King Ferdinand II of Aragon and Queen Isabella I of Castile. The marriage of these sovereigns and the 'establishment of consistent policies' in their respective kingdoms paved the way for the eventual creation of a unified Kingdom of Spain.

The events that conspired to bring these three people together go back to 1453, when the Turks captured Constantinople, thereby taking control of the overland trade route between the Mediterranean eastwards to India and China. Western traders were keen to discover other routes, and Columbus was one of several people who were up for the challenge. The dangers were considerable, but then, so were the rewards.

Columbus's brother, Bartolomeo, was a cartographer, so had first-hand knowledge of the contemporary views on geography. Equipped with this information, adding to it from what he read in books and with an unshakeable faith in himself and in God, Columbus sought an audience with King John II of Portugal, who was interested in exploring ideas to increase competitiveness in trade. The king's enthusiasm waned, however, when experts reported (correctly) that Columbus had underestimated the distance between the West Coast of Europe and the 'land beyond the sea'. When the Portuguese navigator Bartolomeu Dias returned to Portugal after successfully having rounded the southern tip of Africa, King John decided not to support Columbus in his attempt to sail off in the opposite direction. Columbus wasn't one to give up easily, and decided to seek an audience with the King and Queen of Spain instead. He met with them for the first time in 1487. They referred to their committees of experts, who returned a sceptical verdict, but Queen Isabella's confessor advised them to keep their options open, so to mitigate the risk of him going elsewhere while they considered his offer, they gave Columbus a retainer and a pass allowing him free food and lodging anywhere he chose to go in Spain.

His patience was rewarded in the end. Columbus's persuasive rhetoric, combined with inflows to the treasury as a result of the campaigns against the Moors and Jews, and the zealous desire to bring more souls into the Christian faith helped the King and Queen make up their minds. On 17 April 1492, outside Granada, they signed an agreement now known as the *Capitulations of Santa Fe*. Columbus was able to fit out three ships and set sail on a voyage that was to change the face of the world as they knew it.

Explore further

For an overview of Spain's history, see Charles Chapman's *A History of Spain* (B21). The section on the era of the Catholic rulers can be found at pages 202–233.

For more information on Columbus, see John Thacher's *Christopher Columbus* (B125), and the recent reassessments of his life by David Sarfaty (*Columbus Re-Discovered*) (B111) and Miles Davidson (*Columbus Then and Now: A Life Reexamined*) (B29).

Never Man

16 August 1940—Sir Winston Churchill visits the RAF Bunker at Uxbridge during the Battle of Britain.

16 August 1940. The world has been in a state of war for nearly a year – some would say even longer. Churchill took over from Neville Chamberlain in May. Chamberlain resigned when the Allies failed to stop the Germans from occupying Norway. Allied forces in France, Belgium, the Netherlands and Luxembourg have been forced to retreat, leading to a mass evacuation from

Dunkirk. Russia is moving from a position of cooperation with Germany to one of hostility towards it. Hitler and Mussolini have put plans in motion to expand into France and Africa. Their plan to invade Britain was announced on 10 June. The Battle of Britain has unfolded in the weeks since. The main battles have been fought in the skies, with heavy losses inflicted and suffered by the RAF.

The Battle of Britain is now at its height. At the RAF training bases in Uxbridge, Northolt, and elsewhere, teams drawn in turn from the thousands of trainees that go through the base every week are being equipped with walkie-talkie R/T sets which are strapped to their uniforms and riding around on modified tricycles fitted with compasses. They're learning how to manoeuvre and process commands given at high speed under stressful conditions.

Below ground, at Uxbridge, in a concrete bunker, a small team of senior officers and strategists directs the British air offensive. The country's under attack. We're defending our freedom, our way of life.

As Churchill emerges from the bunker, he's visibly moved, and from that emotional moment comes the line, "Never in the field of human conflict has so much been owed by so many to so few."

Accompanying him is his Chief Staff Officer, Hastings Lionel Ismay, 1st Baron Ismay, on whose advice Churchill has come to rely heavily over the past year.

Later, Churchill works the line into a speech he plans to give in the House of Commons, on 20 August.

Ismay, whose nickname was 'Pug', later recalled that Churchill, discussing the speech with him, had used a different form: "Never in the history of mankind have so many owed so much to so few", upon which Ismay asked, "What about Jesus and his disciples?" Winston's answer was, "Good old Pug," and the 'Never in the field of human conflict … ' wording was used in a speech which went down in history as the 'Never in the field of human conflict' speech.

The title of this riddle refers to a passage from another speech of Churchill's which became famous. He delivered it at his old school, Harrow, on 29 October 1941. It contained these lines, which use repetition, contraction and expansion masterfully to elucidate a point:

> Never give in. Never give in. Never, never, never – in nothing, great or small, large or petty – never give in, except to convictions of honour and good sense. Never yield to force; never yield to the apparently overwhelming might of the enemy.

It is particularly poignant to read through the speech, in light of his comments on one word of a new verse added to the school song in his honour.

Churchill has featured highly in lists of notable British achievers, but has not gone uncriticised for his racist remarks, in particular his attitude to Indian politics. Churchill was human. He made mistakes. When he confessed them, he did so while brushing them aside with humour. When he admitted to having to eat his own words, he added, "… I must confess that I have always found them a healthy diet."

Outside his political career, during which he held a variety of posts, Churchill was an artist, a prolific author who received the Nobel Prize for Literature, an active bricklayer, and a lepidopterist.

Explore further

Trainee pilots really did dart around on specially modified tricycles – you can explore this phenomenon further in Chapter 3 of Flight Lieutenant Tony 'Plez' Pleasant's memoirs published on The Association of Royal Air Force Fighter Control Officers website (C59).

A transcript of the speech Churchill gave at Harrow in 1941 can be found on The Churchill Centre website (C19). Various views of his alleged racism can be found in an article by Mark Burdman in *Executive Intelligence Review* (A5) and documents on the Churchill Centre website (C4, C42).

For an annotated scholarly selection of the top 10 biographies on Churchill published up to 2005, see Paul Addison's selection published on *The Guardian* website (C2), which is headed up by Churchill's own account: *My Early Life* (B24). A notable work from the period which does not appear on his list is *The Last Lion* trilogy by William Manchester and Paul Reid (B71). More recently, Jonathan Rose (B109), Lawrence James (B54) and Carlo d'Este (B28) have attempted to cast new light on Churchill's life and times.

Pine Tree

Pompeii, 79 CE—The eruption of Vesuvius.

The letter was written by the historian Pliny the Younger, about events that happened when he was 18 years old. It describes the death of his uncle, Pliny the Elder, as a result of trying to help others escape the effects of a major natural disaster: the eruption of the active volcano known as Vesuvius in 79 CE.

Twenty-five years later, Pliny was asked by the historian Tacitus to set down his memories of the event, alongside eyewitness accounts of his uncle's death.

At the time, Pliny the Elder was living at Misenum (now Miseno), a city around 20 miles away from across the bay from the volcano, in what's now known as the Bay of Naples in present-day Italy. The city derived its name from a story in Virgil's *Aeneid* in which the trumpeter Misenus allegedly drowned at this site after competing in a show of talent against the sea god, Triton. Pliny the Elder was then commander of the Roman fleet. His sister and her son, Pliny (the Younger), had been staying with him.

Minor earthquakes occurred quite regularly. They were part of normal life back then. There had been minor earthquakes prior to the extreme eruption of 79 CE, so nothing out of the ordinary seemed to be happening, and although they happened more frequently than usual, people didn't seem that worried. Pliny the Younger, who had spent his early childhood in the north of Italy near Lake Como, wasn't old enough then to remember when Vesuvius had last erupted, nor had he been in the area then – the last major eruption had been in 62 CE, when he was only one, with a lesser eruption in 64 CE, when the emperor Nero had been giving a performance which he insisted on finishing before the theatre was evacuated. It collapsed shortly afterwards.

All this, for them, was a long time ago and people were getting on with restoring the city.

From across the bay, the family noticed a column of smoke rising from a mountain. Pliny the Elder, wanting to investigate the phenomenon at close hand, ordered a boat to be made ready. He offered his nephew the opportunity of going with him, but the younger Pliny refused, deciding to stay behind instead and complete a writing exercise his uncle had set him. Just as Pliny the Elder was leaving his house, he received a message from a friend asking him to bring a ship across the bay to save them, as they had none and had no other means of escape. On receiving the message, he decided to call out the fleet, ordering the triremes to head for the coast and evacuate people, while he took a lighter sailing vessel to try to rescue his friends. The wind was blowing towards the coast and his ship was unable to leave. Clouds of ash dropped debris of rock and pumice down on them. His helmsman urged him to turn back, but Pliny the Elder said, "Fortune favours the brave," and ordered him on, dictating his observations of the conditions to a shipmate to record as they approached land. Pliny the Elder disembarked, sought out his friends, spent the evening with them, then followed his normal routine of bathing, sleeping and waking. The next morning, the eruptions started to get worse, and he deemed it sensible that they try to evacuate.

The eruptions lasted for two whole days, with alternate explosions of ash and molten lava, accompanied by earthquakes and a minor tsunami at one point. Some people sought the shelter of buildings, others headed for open spaces. Pliny the Elder and his friends were among these. They'd tied pillows to their heads for protection against falling rocks and taken torches with them to help them see through the cloud of thick, black ash. They made it to the coast, but although others escaped, Pliny the Elder collapsed, either as a result of an existing weakness or a severe reaction to the sulphurous fumes from the volcano which had just been released.

It is estimated that over the two days, the volcano released the equivalent of 1.5 million tonnes of solid matter per second, killing an estimated 16,000 people, not to mention animals and livestock, burying the towns of Pompeii and Heraclaneum completely.

A chance discovery of one of the houses in Pompeii occurred in 1599, but the significance of the find was missed and the site was covered over. Serious excavations of Pompeii and the surrounding areas began in 1748 as a result of discoveries made when Spanish architects began to dig the foundations for a palace for Charles III of Spain who had conquered Naples, adding the title of 'King of Naples' to his name. Pompeii has become one of Italy's most popular tourist destinations.

Vesuvius remains an active volcano. While the 79 CE eruption was the worst known to date, several others have occurred between then and now. In 1906, damage resulting from an eruption made plans to hold the 1908 Olympics in Naples impossible and London was chosen to host the games instead. The last major eruption was in 1944.

The collapse of several structures in an excavated area of Pompeii between 2010 and 2012, mainly due to heavy rainfall, raised concerns about conservation and preservation of the exposed areas. At the time of writing, the site is being assessed for inclusion on UNESCO's list of World Heritage Sites in Danger.

Explore further

The primary sources on which this riddle is based include Pliny's letters to Baebius Macer and Tacitus (B92 – *Letters 27, 65*), Suetonius' *Life of Nero* (B121 – Volume 2, pp 86–187) and Tacitus' *Annals* (B122 – Book 15, Chapter 22).

You can follow the progress of the application to include Pompeii on UNESCO's list of World Heritage Sites in Danger on the UNESCO website (C12). And if you're wondering about why Pompeii is sometimes referred to with one terminal *'i'* and sometimes two, the convention is that the ancient town takes two and the modern region takes one, although this is not followed on the UNESCO website. More in-depth information on Pompeii can be found in the printed and online resources produced to accompany the 2013 British Museum exhibition, *Life and death in Pompeii and Herculaneum* (B106, C45).

Revolt

The coast of Gaul, 43 CE—The Emperor Claudius prepares to invade Britannia.

The commander of the Roman army depicted here is Aulus Plautius (first century CE) who oversaw the invasion and conquest of Britain during the reign of the Emperor Claudius (10 BCE–54 CE). The campaign was mounted ostensibly to reinstate the ousted ruler, Verica, who was recognised as King of Britain by the Romans, and who may have lived in Fishbourne, in West Sussex, where the largest Roman home in Britain, as far as we know, was built shortly after the invasion. There's a museum there now, which you can visit.

According to Suetonius, Claudius, having been offered the

trappings of a triumph by the senate without having done anything to deserve them, thought it would be beneath his dignity to accept, but looked around for an easy victory and his eye fell on Britain. The timing was perfect. Instead of reinstating Verica, he took over himself, stayed there for 6 months and returned to claim his triumph in Rome. Sources disagree as to whether the troops crossed from East to West, departing from Boulogne (Gessoriacum) and landing at Richborough on the Kent coast, or from South to North, landing near Fishbourne. Whether Narcissus' show was really a comedy is debatable. According to Dio, the soldiers called off their mutiny when they experienced something that made them react as if at a Saturnalia. Dio could have been describing the event with a touch of Senecan irony. His previous mentions of Narcissus as Claudius' right-hand man depict him as a ruthless and seditious executioner, rather than a liberal adviser. Given this, the show he put on could very well have been the very opposite of humourous – so bad, in fact, that the army had no choice but to laugh in the face of extreme adversity. As far as I know, no one to date has come up with a definitive answer. There's no reason why *you* shouldn't give it a go. As with many of these riddles, the account is intended to provoke informed discussion and debate about key events in history. What kind of show do *you* think it might have been?

Explore further

This riddle is based on the account in Cassius Dio's *Roman History* (B25 – Book 60, Chapters 19–23, Volume 7, pp 414–427) and Suetonius' account of *The Deified Claudius* (B121 – Book 5, Chapter 17, Volume 2, pp 34–35).

At the time of Claudius' conquest, Britain was inhabited by 27 tribes which you can find out more about on the BBC History website (C55). Verica was the leader of the Atrebate tribe.

A brief outline of theories on the possible landing site of the Roman troops and the development and history of the Roman palace at Fishbourne can be found in Dave Musgrove's *100 Places That Made Britain* (B83 – pp 10–13).

Revolution

Paris, 1789—Marie Tussaud prepares to take a plaster cast of Marie Antoinette's head to create a wax figure from it for public display.

Some artistic license has been taken with this riddle as there is a lack of clarity regarding the method by which casts of people's heads were made and when. Marie Tussaud is known to have created wax models of both King Louis XVI and Queen Marie Antoinette from life prior to the revolution. Marie's great-grandson, John Tussaud, states that she did not witness Marie Antoinette's execution, although he mentions that hers was one of the heads she was compelled to create by the National Assembly.

To what extent she was ordered to make wax models of heads severed by the guillotine against her will and to what extent she sought out the opportunity to do so for commercial gain is unclear. Berridge, one of her biographers, points out that it is possible that Curtius, Tussaud's mentor, struck a deal with the executioner, to allow them access to the victims' heads. One has to take into account the fact that the ethos appeal of the first story of Tussaud being the unwilling victim, compelled to carry out a gruesome deed, is far greater than that of the second, in which she and Curtius actively sought out the opportunity to take advantage of the situation in which they found themselves. The stories should be considered alongside the conflicting evidence that Berridge presents about the incarceration of the Tussaud family with Joséphine de Beauharnais (which made a good story, but Berridge argues is at least unlikely), and the refashioning of Tussaud's image after her death. The story of her being forced to create wax effigies circulated around Paris at the time – whether as an urban legend, or a true story is up to you to decide.

Although the question of how Marie Tussaud gained access to the heads she modelled remains open, it does seem that in certain cases – with Marat, or the heads of Robespierre; Madame Elizabeth, the King's sister; or particularly in the case of that of her close friend, the Princesse de Lamballe, according to Mrs Adams-Acton's testimony, for one – Tussaud did work with freshly butchered heads and bodies, and did not do so unfeelingly. This riddle is inspired jointly by this latter case and Tussaud's own account of her reaction to the sight of Marie Antoinette on the way to her execution.

Berridge's account puts Tussaud's exhibition very much in the context of its time, a time when people-watching was a national recreation – from the rituals at court, during which the queen would take her morning bath and breakfast in front of a large audience of courtiers, to her appearances at the theatre, where people would be seriously injured in their attempts to climb over each other to get a close look at the latest creation of hair or fashion she was sporting so that they could copy it the next day. Waxworks gave the general public an insight into that world in safer and more informal surroundings. These waxwork shows did not emerge out of nothing, for precedents existed in the world of fashion, where wax dolls were used to model collections in the miniature.

In the early days of the revolution, wax heads borrowed from Curtius's exhibition were borrowed so that they could be paraded down the streets of Paris, perhaps in a grotesque mockery of religious processions. It should be remembered that not only was the relationship between the head and the body seen to symbolise the relationship between the rational and the bestial at the time, the separation of both was a spiritual as well as a temporal assassination.

Unfortunately, the far-from-pious event contributed to a mounting lust for blood, with children decapitating cats and parading their heads down the streets in imitation of the behaviour of their elders. Paradoxically, the practice of making wax votive offerings as part of Catholic devotional practice was widespread.

During the worst days of the revolution, what Curtius and Tussaud offered was a substitute ritual, which was encouraged by the powers that be in the spirit of crowd control – the Romans used bread and circuses; the French, short of bread, offered wax models in the hope that they would satisfy both needs.

As an aside, Marie-Antoinette's dog, Coco, survived her execution, ending up in the Hapsburg court in Austria after having spent some time living in the prison where his mistress had been incarcerated. With the restoration of Bourbon monarchy, he returned to Paris, dying shortly after. Coco is buried in the grounds of the Hôtel de Seignelay, once a magnificent private residence located at 80 rue de Lille in the seventh arrondissement – a stone's throw from the spot where Marie-Antoinette was beheaded.

Explore further

The main primary source for the life of Madame Tussaud is the Tussaud-Hervé (auto)biography (B130). Secondary sources include her great-grandson's account of her life (B129), along with more recent works by Berridge (B13) and by Chapman (B22), among others, as well as several fictional works, of which Michelle Moran's *Madame Tussaud* is an example (B79). Mrs Adams-Acton's testimony is quoted in Berridge, *op cit*, p 92.

You can read more about Marie Antoinette's dog, Coco, in Paris-based author Matthew Fraser's blog post about her (C74). A picture of Coco's gravestone can be found on Wikimedia (C70).

Sealed

Runnymede, England, 19 June 1215—King John is made to set his seal to The Barons' Charter *(known since 1217 as the* Magna Carta*).*

In this scene, we're at Runnymede, a field where meetings – particularly meetings of the Witan, the wise members of the Council of Anglo-Saxon Kings – have been held for 400 years, hence the name (see **Sealed** clues, page [pp]).

It's some gathering. The people involved are King John of England (also known as John Lackland); Master Pandulph, the Papal legate; Prince Llewellyn the Great of Wales; Alexander II King of the Scots; 25 Anglo-Norman barons; a representative of the Knights Templar; 2 archbishops; 10 bishops; and 20 abbots. If not all present, they have all been involved in drawing up the document which is placed in front of the king. Some are the king's advisers; others are rebels. All of them want the king to put his seal to the document.

What's the document? It's a list of demands compiled by twenty-five dissatisfied barons, witnessed by others – including royalty and clergy, all of whom want to bring the king to order.

The entire assembled company, advisers and rebels alike, is keen for the king to honour its terms in order to maintain stability and justice within the kingdom.

The meeting in June 1215 has been a long time coming. King John has been putting it off for quite a while.

In July the previous year, King John had lost Normandy to King Philip II of France, after a rather costly battle. He wasn't best pleased when he heard the news. Apparently pouring money at the venture was not enough. Who did the king blame? Himself? His generals? His soldiers? Fate? Apparently he blamed God. He's reputed to have said, "Since I became reconciled to God, and submitted myself and my kingdoms to the Church of Rome, woe is me, nothing has gone prosperously with me ..."

This takes the story back to at least 1205.

When Hubert Walter, Archbishop of Canterbury died, the laws regarding who should choose the next archbishop were unclear. The archbishop, as the Primate of All England, traditionally occupied the highest position in the Church in England hierarchy, making it an important political and cultural post.

King John, who believed he had the right to appoint a successor, favoured John de Grey, Bishop of Norwich. The canons of Canterbury Cathedral, who believed the right to appoint fell to them, chose Reginald, their Sub-Prior. Both parties sent delegates to Rome to obtain the Pope's blessing and have him confirm their choice. Pope Innocent III, overruling both parties as head of the Church, chose neither John de Grey nor Reginald, but appointed Cardinal Stephen Langton to the post, a candidate of his own choosing, whom he knew personally.

A power struggle followed. King John refused to acknowledge the Pope's authority in this matter and forbade Langton and the Canterbury delegation to enter the country. In retaliation, the Pope issued an interdict on England in 1207. This meant that no weddings or communion rites were allowed to take place. An exception was made for baptisms, confessions, and absolutions for the dying. King John wasn't happy about this and countered by declaring that any church bodies who obeyed the Pope's instructions would have their property confiscated. Fearing his subjects would start a rebellion, as these policies affected them directly, and created a rift between their spiritual and material interests, he took members of the key noble families hostage to try to ensure they enforced order as his feudal vassals. In 1209, the Pope retaliated by excommunicating King John. The king eventually relented and allowed the Archbishop of Canterbury and his monks to return to England as a gesture of good faith. However, he refused to reimburse the Pope any of the monies he had gained from the church property he had confiscated. In 1211, the Pope responded by releasing the English people from their allegiance to their King.

Around this time, King John was fighting wars in Ireland and Wales to secure and expand his territories there. He wanted to regain the lands he had lost on the Continent in 1204. He was also supporting William, King of the Scots, against local insurrections. He had to pull back from both Welsh and continental attacks in 1212 to fend off a rebellion headed up in the main by two dissatisfied Anglo-Norman nobles, Robert Fitzwalter and Eustace de Vesci (William, King of the Scots' son-in-law).

In order to fund the campaigns he had been fighting since his accession, King John had to raise funds. His main sources of income were *scutage* (payments to avoid military service), *tallage* (taxes raised from the Jewish community – sometimes, it would appear, through torture), and the sale of favours. Income from royal estates played a smaller part.

In 1213, King John sought a new resolution with the Pope. The king officially devolved power to the Pope in return for a set sum of money to be paid to the king annually by the Pope. He also agreed, in principle, to pay the church compensation for income lost during the interdiction years. In practice, he stalled on fulfilling his part of the bargain for as long as he could.

Why the sudden about-turn? According to Roger of Wendover, King John was simply buying himself time and resources. He was planning to invade France, but couldn't rely on the support of his nobles unless he was absolved. When Stephen, Archbishop of Canterbury, arrived in England, John made sure he was there to meet him. The king prostrated himself in front of the archbishop who granted him absolution on the condition that the king swore to uphold the laws of the land. He did and was duly absolved. But what were the laws? And how could the king be made to keep his word?

On 25 August 2014, the Archbishop of Canterbury brought Henry I of England's *Charter of Liberties* to the barons' attention at St Paul's in London and proposed that they should get King John to honour these existing rights, and oppose him by force if they were unable to get him to agree to do so. This decision led directly to the composition of the *Barons' Charter*. In response to continued prevarication by King John, a group of barons sought to gain tactical positions from which to defy the king. They turned towards London. The city let them in. Other centres of baronial strengths such as Northampton went over to their side. To buy time, King John agreed to meet the barons at Runnymede, where he finally set his seal to their charter.

The charter was copied and distributed around the country. Four copies of the document are still in existence. However, the original text of the *Barons' Charter* did not appear in literary sources until 1759. As William Sharp McKechnie points out, Roger of Wendover's account cited Henry II's confirmed version which contained 37 clauses, as opposed to the 61 clauses of the 1215 version. The later, shorter version was the first version to enter into English law.

At Runnymede, King John set his seal to the *Barons' Charter*. A shorter charter, called *Carta Libertatum* (The Charter of Liberties), was presented to the 9-year-old Henry III (or rather William Marshal, the regent) after John's death in 1216. This was called *Magna Carta Libertatum* (The Great Charter of Liberties) to distinguish it from the separate *Carta de Foresta* (The Forest Charter) issued in 1217. They were both joined in 1225, when they became part of statutory law. They were reissued by Edward I in 1297 as the *Confirmation Cartarum* (Confirmation of Charters). The ping-pong game of power-wielding continued, with Pope Clement V promptly annulling the charter in 1305.

Three of the original sixty-one clauses are still in force today and the Magna Carta is seen as a landmark of legal and constitutional history in its attempt to limit the powers of the ruling monarch, and setting the law as the foremost power in the land.

Most importantly, a clause which states that 25 barons acting in agreement and following the legal practice of *distraint* can depose a ruling monarch if they are found to be acting outside the law.

Almost immediately, the king – understandably, perhaps – moved to renege on the agreement. He argued that he had been forced into setting his seal to it against his will and that the powers it gave the barons over him went against the sovereign powers that he had given over to the Pope in 1213. Pope Innocent III agreed, announced his support for King John and excommunicated the rebel barons, an act which, among other factors, led to the First Barons' War (1215–1217).

The barons offered their allegiance to Prince Louis of France, who had fought under his father, King Philip, against King John, in 1204. They invited him to become King of England. The Pope wasn't happy about this, neither was King Philip at first; but Louis, secure in the support of the barons, having taken hostages in case of trouble, and probably keen to earn his spurs and gain territory of his own, eventually got his father's blessing and crossed the channel with a large force. He occupied London peacefully and was acclaimed king at St Paul's (though never crowned). He went on to attack and occupy Essex, Suffolk, Norfolk, Norwich Castle and York. He also gained power over most of Northumberland, then laid siege to Dover and Windsor Castles and captured Cambridge Castle. King John retaliated, punishing the rebel barons by razing their lands around Windsor, then went on to devastate more of their lands in Norfolk and Suffolk. He did the same to their lands around Dover, although Louis occupied Dover Castle. When crossing the river Wellester, King John lost the possessions he carried with him, including the royal regalia. He became sick, travelled on to Newark and died there, on 18 October 1216. On his deathbed, he appointed his son, Henry III, his successor.

Henry III was crowned in Gloucester Cathedral. The barons, having learned of a plan that Louis had to banish all the traitorous barons from the country once he had gained power, decided to switch sides and swear their allegiance to Henry III, as long as he swore to uphold the laws King John had agreed to in the Barons' Charter.

William Marshal, the regent, supported this and saw it as an important move to maintain peace and stability within the country. The defeat of Louis's forces at Lincoln, Dover and Sandwich in 1217 by the English led to the Treaty of Lambeth in which Louis agreed to renounce his claim to the English throne and recognise Henry III as the lawful king. Louis left England on

28 September 1217 with 10,000 marks as compensation. The rebel barons were granted amnesty, and he agreed not to mount another attack on England. Peace was finally restored.

The *Magna Carta* is hailed as a major point in the history of the development of civil society, in its laying out of basic rights and freedoms, as well as the status of a ruler by divine right in relation to the law.

The issue, however, is not as clear-cut as some historians would like it to be. As the case of Louis shows, while public opinion may be enough to elect a president, it is not enough to elect a monarch. British monarchs are still consecrated as part of the highly symbolic liturgical coronation rite. While the role of the monarch is largely constitutional today, the monarch is still the head of the Church of England, and holds the titles of *Fidei Defensor* (Defender of the Faith), originally granted by the Pope to Henry VIII in 1526, and confirmed by parliament after the reformation; and the style *Dei Gratia* (by the grace of God [D.G.]) for some a historical formula, for others a reminder of the subservience of the absolute will of a monarch to a higher power. The paradoxical balance is reflected to this day in the continued use of *Dieu et mon droit* (God and my right) as the royal motto. The motto was coined by Richard the Lionheart, King John's older brother, at the Battle of Gisors in 1193, acknowledging no higher power but God, alongside his divine right to rule as monarch. The subtle maintenance of the balance of power between monarch, subjects and the higher power to which both are subject remains the keystone of the institution which is the British monarchy to this day.

The complex way in which the rule of law runs alongside symbolic currents of tradition, custom, convention and heritage which contribute – often paradoxically, yet mysteriously harmoniously – to the elusive thing we call contemporary British culture is an aspect of British cultural heritage which is all too often sadly underestimated and unappreciated.

Explore further

The main primary source for this event is the account given in Roger of Wendover's *Flowers of History* (B108 – Volume 2, pp 215 ff). King John's *Concession of England to the Pope* can be found in Stubb's *Charters* (A23 – pp 430–431).

Further information on the history of confusion about the documents which constituted the original *Magna Carta* can be found in William Sharp McKechnie's commentary on the work (B76 – pp 176 ff). The history of its acceptance into legal code can be found in Frederic Maitland's *The Constitutional History of England* (B70 – p 16). For those interested in pursuing the legal aspects of the *Magna Carta* and the British Constitution further, a good starting point for an exploration of the relationship between the rule of law and the role of a monarch can be found in Bracton's *De legibus et consuetudinibus Angliae (On the Laws and Customs of England)* compiled between 1220 and 1250, available in modern English on line (C15).

Shells

The coast of Gaul, 39/40 CE—Caligula's soldiers stop to gather seashells on the beach, during his planned campaign to invade Britain. This riddle's written from the viewpoint of a fictional soldier in Caligula's army. While the soldier's used as a literary device, the scenes he describes are all based on classical historical accounts of Caligula's campaign to conquer Britain.

Fear. Hatred. Power. These are the most common themes associated with Caligula's reign. He was unpredictable, extreme in his behaviour, hugely extravagant, avaricious, allegedly incestuous and lascivious. As emperor, he gradually manipulated himself into a position of power that made him almost untouchable, terrorising Rome until he was assassinated. But the record of the early years of his reign tells a different story. What caused the change? Was it a sudden seismic shift from good to bad or was it a gradual change? If he was really insane, were there moments of lucidity that broke through the clouds of insane behaviour? Or was there calculated method behind the real or apparent madness? And why, in 39 CE, did Caligula decide to go to war? Why was it important for him to show he could win a battle? And why Britannia?

Perhaps it was a tactical decision. After all, he'd won over the emperor Tiberius somehow. Tiberius killed Caligula's mother and brothers, but adopted Caligula; grooming him for succession and indulging his vices. In managing to survive in this situation, despite claims that he had killed Tiberius, he had shown himself to be a shrewd tactician, so it is possible that when it came to battle, he combined his strategic skills with his tactical ones and concluded that it would be better – and safer – to stage a victory than try to win one. And seeing as he was keen that people believed he was a god, he could very well have wanted to make sure he was victorious. If he believed this himself, though, would he have been so devious in the staging of the outcomes of his campaigns? The accounts raise more questions than they answer.

Perhaps the motivation was financial. According to Cassius Dio, prior to his military campaigns in Germania and this aborted campaign to invade Britannia, he'd accused a large number of senators of crimes against the state, spent a huge amount of money on constructing a pontoon bridge across the Bay of Baiae (also known as the Bay of Bauli) on the western coast of Italy, just to prove a soothsayer wrong, among other private and public projects, which left him short of cash. While he did raise money through threats and sequestration, plunder would have been another potential source of income. Perhaps, as Dio claims, the 'little bootie' (which is what Caligula's name means in Latin) went to war just to get some more booty.

Perhaps the motivation was vanity. Caligula's sea-crossing exploit was, according to Dio, a direct response to the senate's decision, motivated by fear, to give him the right to celebrate an ovation (an honour much less impressive than a triumph, but usually given as a result of a minor victory). It could be that Caligula wanted a triumph and this was a means of getting one.

Whatever the reason, in 39 CE, Caligula set out on a sightseeing tour to see the famed beauty spot at the north end of the Via Flaminia, where the source of the river Clitumnus was located. From there, having recruited an army, he went on to quell a rebellion in Germania.

Whether he'd experienced imperial comfort growing up alongside the army as a boy, or whether he'd experienced a more Spartan style of living; as emperor, he viewed the soldier's life with disdain. When he did set out, he did so in unpredictable style and unprecedented comfort, according to both Dio and Suetonius.

In Germania, Suetonius tells us that he received an embassy from the British king, Adminius, who had been driven out of Britain by his father, Cunobeline. Caligula, having staged a battle in Germany, set off for Britain, it would seem, as a result of this meeting. When he arrived at the coast of Gaul, he ordered his soldiers to gather up shells, as 'spoils of the ocean', then marched back to Rome with his army, sending news of his victory over the Germans ahead of him. Suetonius' account has inspired the interpretation that Caligula waged war against Neptune. This view was popularised by the prolific novelist and classicist Robert Graves in *I, Claudius*. It is inferred, in part perhaps, from the statement in Dio's account, that Caligula – who, according to Suetonius, could not swim – claimed that Neptune was afraid of him, when seeing the seas stayed calm when he crossed the Bay of Baiae. Apparently he never crossed the channel.

Sextus Aurelius Victor, who says that the Greeks, being prone to exaggeration, saw 'cockles' as nymphs' eyes, deduces from that that they were gathered as a sign of triumph over the domain of the sea gods. However, the link between Caligula dressing up as Venus and the importance of seashells to her image is given prominence by the American Classical scholar, Chad Schroeder, who argues that the whole scene was an act of political propaganda, rather than an act of madness. David Woods infers a different link between cockles, and Caligula's order. He prefers to interpret the Greek text as meaning 'coracles' – small boats that are likened to hollow shells, in the same sense as 'cockles' can be applied to both boats and shells in modern English; but cites other scholars who believe that the reference to shells (a) referred to small huts or containers implying female genitalia, and was used in a euphemistic sense to convey the notion that Caligula allowed his soldiers to visit brothels, or that (b) it meant the soldiers used the shells as missiles for target practice in drills, with yet others building on that view, believing that (c) Caligula ordered the exercise to humiliate his soldiers. In a more eruditely researched paper, Marleen Flory, another American classical scholar, links Caligula's actions with Julius Caesar's 100 years previously, noting the fact that Caesar had given a cuirass made entirely of pearls culled from the English Channel to the statue of Venus in the temple of Venus Genetrix, and that Caesar's conquest of Britannia was subsequently celebrated in literature using a trope which claimed his victory was also a 'conquest of the ocean', giving a cultural reference for Caligula's actions, which she interprets literally, that may have been twisted by later historians, none of whom looked particularly favourably on Caligula, however balanced their writings may seem to be on the surface.

Explore further

Suetonius' account of Caligula's life (B121 – Book 4, Chapter 46 – Volume 1, pp 474–477) provides the main inspiration for the content of this riddle, with elements like descriptions of Caligula embarking on his trireme taken from Cassius Dio Cocceianus' *Roman History* (B25 – Book 59, Chapter 25, Volume 7, pp 336–341) and his dressing up as Venus from Sextus Aurelius Victor's *The Caesars* (B133 – Book 3, Lines 11/12 – pp 3/4). Other classical sources for Caligula's life include Philo Judaeus (A24 – Book 6, pp 107–108) and Josephus (A13 – Books 18–19, pp 470 ff).

If you're interested in exploring Caligula's character further, you might find it interesting to compare classical authors' accounts with the accounts of more recent historians such as Anthony Barrett's *Caligula: The Corruption of Power* (B10), or Aloys Winterling's *Caligula: A Biography* (B146).

The articles referred to above on the question of why Caligula might have ordered his soldiers to gather up seashells by Marleen Flory (A14), David Woods (A51) and Chad Schroeder (C68) are worth looking at if you want to explore this aspect of the story further. I hope they inspire you to come up with your own theory.

Stand Up!

Montgomery, Alabama, USA, 1 December 1955—Rosa Parks is arrested for refusing to comply with state legislation regarding segregation on local buses.

On Thursday, 1 December 1955, Rosa Parks was arrested for refusing to give up her seat to a white person on a city bus in Montgomery, Alabama when requested to do so by the driver.

The arrest led to a mass boycott of the city bus company which lasted for 183 days, which became one of the key events in the civil rights movement in the US.

Rev Martin Luther King, Jr., described the 'Great Decision' shortly afterwards in these words:

> The bus protest is not merely in protest of the arrest of Mrs. Rosa Parks, but is the culmination of a series of unpleasant incidents over a period of years. It is an upsurging of a ground swell which has been going on for a long time. Our cup of tolerance has run over. Thousands of our people, who have had unhappy experiences, prefer to walk rather than endure more. No better evidence can be given that the fact that a large percent of the Negro bus riders are now walking or getting a ride whenever and wherever they can.

At that time, segregation was legal and the responsibility for setting the limits of white and coloured sections (as they were then designated) was given to the drivers. There seems to have been an understanding that the front 10 seats were designated as the white section, and that some drivers would seek to extend that section by a row if white people were left standing. While they were not legally supposed to relocate passengers unless there were seats available for them to sit in, many drivers wittingly or unwittingly ignored this directive. Some drivers also insisted that black passengers pay them their fare at the front of a crowded bus, then dismount and reboard the bus via the back door to enter the coloured section, rather than disturb the whites. Drivers were then known to drive on before black passengers who had paid their fare were able to reboard.

For Parks, on that day, a combination of factors seems to have led to her decision:

- Attitudes towards segregation had changed significantly after World War II, when black soldiers had fought side by side with their white compatriots as equal citizens and been treated as such outside the US, but not on their return.
- As a political activist, she would have been aware of recent changes. These included the desegregation of interstate buses in 1946 (see below), of postgraduate education in Texas in 1950, and of the public schooling system in 1954.
- There had been precedents locally and in other states in which women had refused to give up their seats on local buses in protest against discriminatory practices (see below).
- She had previously had an unpleasant experience with that particular bus driver, who had driven off without her after she had paid her fare and had to dismount to reboard the bus.
- While she had gone out of her way following that incident not to board a bus he was driving, on this occasion she had

not checked, and only realised once she had paid her fare.
- She had recently attended a class in which non-violent protest action was discussed as a legitimate way to tackle discrimination.

As noted above, before Rosa Parks' arrest, there had been others.

Irene Morgan had been arrested in 1944 for refusing to move to another seat on an interstate bus when requested to do so by the driver. The driver had chosen to uphold state segregation laws when passing through Virginia. Her arrest, trial and appeal resulted in a ruling to desegregate interstate bus routes in 1946.

It took a while for this to filter down from legislation into practice, however.

On 1 August 1952, Sarah Keys was arrested in similar circumstances to Morgan's on a Carolina Trailways vehicle travelling between Washington DC and Washington, North Carolina as part of an interstate journey which had started in Fort Dix, New Jersey. Her court hearings lasted three years, ending in a ruling which restated the view that segregation subjected interstate passengers to 'unjust discrimination and undue and unreasonable prejudice and disadvantage' – a judgement passed on 7 November 1955, less than a month before Rosa Parks refused to move from her seat on her local bus.

Eight months prior to Parks' arrest, however, on 2 March 1955, Claudette Colvin was arrested in similar circumstances to Parks', on a local bus in Montgomery, but was additionally charged with assault, which she denied.

In June 1955, three months after Colvin's arrest, Lucille Times had a fight with a Montgomery bus driver, after he had tried to force her car off the road and into a ditch. She took the story to the then head of the Montgomery Chapter of the National Association for the Advancement of Coloured People (NAACP), ED Nixon, suggesting they boycott the buses. She'd witnessed the boycott of a grocery store in Detroit when visiting relatives, and knew what a powerful tool it could be for political activism. Nixon advised her to bide her time. Impatient for action, however, she started to offer lifts to anyone who would take them, and continued to provide a taxi service free of charge throughout the boycott once it got underway. She made it a point never to ride a city bus herself thereafter.

The idea wasn't a new one. It had been voiced previously in Montgomery, as a warning, in a letter by Jo Ann Robinson, then president of Montgomery, Alabama's Women's Political Council, to Mayor Gayle dated 21 May 1954.

By December 1955, the time was ripe for action, and Rosa Parks just happened to be the right person in the right place at the right time (or the 'wrong' place, depending on the historical perspective you take).

Barry Schwartz and others have pointed out that Rosa Parks' eagerness to attend classes in political activism, her record of political activism in working to help black people register as voters, and her respectability and community standing made her an ideal candidate to provide a human face for the campaign to end segregation.

The main documents on which this account is based include Parks' police file, the transcript of her trial, and on interviews given by Rosa Parks between 1955 and 1985 (see below). Additional documents are drawn upon to clarify certain aspects of her story.

While the police report stated that Rosa had been sitting in the white section of the bus, when Rosa had boarded the bus, she had taken a seat in the black section. This is something she was keen to emphasise in an early radio interview in April 1955. As she said in an interview she gave in 1983,

> I just didn't *feel* ... that ... *this* type of treatment was due *any* passenger paying equal fare but being treated so unfairly and unequally.

In combination, the figure of Rosa Parks, the Montgomery Bus Boycott, the number of court cases that sought to test the legality of segregation against the principles enshrined in the US Constitution, and the 14th Amendment in particular, together created a force to be reckoned with. It was this force of an unstoppable quest for justice that eventually brought segregation to an end.

The story of Rosa Parks has been told many ways, and its facts often misrepresented. When I first heard the story, it included a memorable line, attributed to Rosa: "Not today." I wish Parks had said it, somehow. It turns out she didn't. I have only been able to trace the line to a secondary source. It appears in Cynthia Kneen's book, *Awake Mind, Open Heart: The Power of Courage and Dignity in Everyday Life*. In her book, Kneen also misrepresents Parks as having not moved because she was tired. Parks eloquently denied this in her own published account which appeared in 1992, 17 years before Kneen's, in which she wrote,

> People always say that I didn't give up my seat because I was tired, but that isn't true. I was not tired physically, or no more tired than I usually was at the end of a working day. I was not old, although some people have an image of me as being old then. I was forty-two. No, the only tired I was, was tired of giving in.

Parks herself raises questions about the place in which she was seated on the bus, stating in a 1985 interview that she made room for her neighbour to get past her when he stood up to vacate his seat. She could only have done so if she had been sitting in the aisle seat. However, in the evidence submitted as part of her trial, she is shown to have been sitting near the window. It is a minor point, and one which probably arises either due to the span of time between the event and the interview, despite the number of times she must have told the story in between, or due to health issues. If, however, on the contrary, it is a correctly remembered part of the story, what does this signify in the light of the original event, of how it was reported then, of its consequences, and of how we relate to it today?

Rosa's relationship with the judiciary only began with her 1954 trial. While she did not take part in *Browder v. Gayle (1956)*, the seminal court case that finally ended segregation on city buses, the case of *Rosa Parks v. LaFace Records, et al. (1999)* was filed on her behalf. The case was settled out of court. After her death, her estate was tied up in a legal dispute between the beneficiaries that resulted in the same outcome as that of *Jarndyce and Jarndyce*, the fictional case featured in Dickens' *Bleak House*.

In 2006, the State of Alabama passed the *Rosa Parks Act*, offering anyone convicted of criminal activity as part of the Montgomery Bus Boycott to apply to have their criminal conviction overturned. The law received mixed reactions.

At the end of the day, any mass demonstration of solidarity is a demonstration of individual conviction. It takes courage to know how to frame the demonstration of that conviction in particular circumstances, but it is particularly heartening when the individual, the communal and the universal unite to support positive, all-integrating change.

There is one document that sums up this unquenchable spirit particularly poignantly in my view, for several reasons. It is the document released by The Montgomery Improvement Association (MIA) on 19 December 1956, following the court ruling in that segregation was no longer legal on state bus routes. Among the many suggestions as to how members of the black community should behave in the 'new world' they were about to inhabit, I quote what I consider to be the most complex in stance:

> If another person is being molested, do not arise to go to his defence, but pray for the oppressor and use moral and spiritual force to carry on the struggle for justice.

The struggle continues today. It's a struggle between the force of individual conviction and the ingrained feelings that result from living in a culture of oppression. It's a struggle that needs to be resolved both within individuals and within society if Alison Murphy's findings – that 50 years on, Montgomery is only partially, not fully integrated – are to be taken seriously. The issue needs to be tackled both directly and vicariously, to eradicate the conditions in which injustice and discrimination are allowed to flourish, wherever and whenever they occur.

Explore further

The address *To The Montgomery Public* which outlined the 'Great Decision' appeared in the Alabama Journal on Christmas day 1955. It's available on line (A46).

The main legal cases relevant to the story, in chronological order, are *Morgan v. Virginia – 328 U.S. 373 (1946)* (C53), *Sweatt v. Painter – 339 U.S. 629 (1950)* (C71), and *Brown v. Board of Education of Topeka – 347 U.S. 483 (1954)* (C16).

The police reports for the arrests of Claudette Colvin (C60) and Rosa Parks (C61) are available on line, as are the documents from Parks' court case (C78). According to Katie McCabe and Dovey Johnson Roundtree (B74 – pp 241/2), the case file for *Sarah Keys v. Carolina Coach Company, 64 MCC 769 (1955)* was destroyed by the US National Archives and Records Administration, but a copy is held in the US Department of Justice Anti-Trust Division, DOJ Case Number 144-54-56. The company is referred to in some sources, including both McCabe and Roundtree's book and *Jet* magazine (A2), as *Carolina Trailways, Inc.*

Parks' and Colvin's stories are told in Parks and Haskins' *Rosa Parks: My Story* (B87) and Phillip Hoose's *Claudette Colvin: Twice Toward Justice* (B48). Various interviews by Rosa Parks can be found on line. The ones referred to in the above account are from *Democracy Now!* (C67), *The Merv Griffin Show* (C57), and *Eyes on the Prize* (C28). Cynthia Kneen's version of Rosa Parks' story can be found in her book, *Awake Mind, Open Heart* (B60).

You can access the document distributed by The Montgomery Improvement Association (MIA) on 19 December 1956 on the Alabama Department of Archives and History website (C73).

Lucille Times' story is told by *Montgomery Advertiser* reporter, Kirsten Barnes, on the Montgomery Bus Boycott website (C13). A facsimile of Jo Ann Robinson's letter recommending boycotting the buses in Montgomery appears in facsimile in her book, *The Montgomery Bus Boycott and the Women Who Started It* (B107 – p viii).

Re-evaluations of the question of how and why Rosa Parks became one of the key symbols of the civil rights movement can be found in Barry Schwartz's *Collective Forgetting and the Symbolic Power of Oneness: The Strange Apotheosis of Rosa Parks* (A41) and Fran O'Malley and Mark Degliobizzi's educational resource for the Delaware Social Studies Education Project (C56).

If you want to find out more about Parks' legacies – both social and material – a good starting point for finding out more about the controversy surrounding the 2006 Rosa Parks Act is an article by Hermene Hartman in The Huffington Post (A20); for racial segregation issues see Alison Murphy's 2009 thesis, *Fifty Years of Challenges to the Colorline: Montgomery, Alabama* (B82) and for the court cases relating to Parks' estate, *Ex Parte Troy University – 961 So.2d 105 (2006)* (C27) and *In Re Estate of Rosa Louise Parks* (C39).

The really fertile ground for further exploration, however, has to do with the conditions which allow injustice and discrimination to happen – and flourish, even – in the first place. Why do you think they are allowed to, and what are the best methods we, as humans, can find and use to eliminate these conditions?

Stars

89 Arch Street, Philadelphia, May 1776—Betsy Ross, her uncle-in-law, George Ross and Colonel George Washington discuss the design of the

proposed flag of the United Colonies.
This riddle evokes the moment when George Washington – then Commander-in-Chief of the Continental Army which represented the Thirteen Colonies that had united to fight for their independence from Great Britain – and George Ross – then delegate from Pennsylvania to Congress, and the woman's uncle-in-law – had come to visit Betsy Ross to ask her to make up a sample for a new flag for the United Colonies. As the story goes, Washington had proposed a design which featured thirteen six-pointed stars on a blue ground, at the top left of a larger design featuring an array of thirteen stripes in an alternating pattern of red and white, but Betsy suggested that five-pointed stars would be better, and the first flag of the United States, which featured the thirteen stars arranged as she envisaged them, in a circle, was born.

The details of this scene are taken from Canby's account of a story handed down through an oral tradition, a hundred years or so after the event. There seems to be general agreement that Betsy Ross was given the contract to produce flags, but her influence on and role in the design of the first flag of the newly formed United States has been questioned.

When the design for the flag was approved by Congress, it was in the manner – as Weaver points out – of ratifying a pre-existent design. Reigart mentions that Ross had previously been employed to make bunting and hangings for public buildings in Philadephia and Columbia as well as naval streamers. It was as a result of this, he claims, that she was approached to manufacture the new flags. He attributes the development of the design to a decorative feature Ross had come up with earlier which was based on Washington's coat of arms.

Weaver agrees with Reigart about Washington's arms being the source for the design. He states that Washington chose a six-pointed star deliberately, thinking it would be easier to cut, but also to differentiate the design from the stars on his coat of arms. If this was so, he doesn't seem to have been very insistent in sticking to his decision.

Weaver elaborates on the source for the colour choice, tentatively putting forward an argument for considering the flag of the Netherlands as a potential source for the inclusion of blue in the new design. If this was the case, it is surely at least equally possible that the 'Red, White and Blue' combination was derived from the Union Flag of Great Britain which was used until 1801, when Saint Patrick's Saltire was added to produce the current design of Great Britain's Union Flag.

In Parry's description of Ross's shop, we are told that her window featured 'the correct forms of the brown and drab bonnets, about whose make-up the women of the Friends' Society were … particular' which may provide a background against which Reigart's comments regarding her use of bold primary colours can be better appreciated.

Affidavits and statements confirming testimony of what can either be described as hearsay or valid records of stories passed down through oral history are included in Parry's work.

The romanticisation of Ross's difficulty of obtaining materials required without being able to raise credit in Canby's account needs to be juxtaposed against the record of her having done previous work for the state in the accounts by Reigart and Parry.

Explore further

The sources on which this riddle is based are Addie Guthrie Weaver's *The Story of Our Flag* (B141), William Canby's paper on *The History of the Flag of the United States* (A6), Colonel John Franklin Reigart's *The History of the First United States Flag* (B104) and Oliver Parry's *Betsy Ross and the United States Flag* (B89).

As to the role that Betsy Ross played in the design of the flag, see Franklin Hanford's *Did Betsey Ross Design the Flag of the United States of America?* (B42).

Washington's arms are illustrated in Weaver (B141 – facing p 15), and if you're curious about how she might have cut a pentagonal star out of paper, and your own experiments with doing that haven't produced the result you want, check out the diagram on page 9 of Weaver's book.

Stop!

Werowocomoco, in the Powhatan tribe's territory, near the current location of Jamestown, Virginia, December 1607—Pocahontas, the Powhatan Chief's daughter, saves the life of the English explorer and adventurer, Captain John Smith.

The riddle is based on the story as John Smith told it in his *Genrall Historie of Virginia, New England & the Summer Isles …* published in 1624. The story doesn't feature in his earlier *A True Relation of Such Occurrences and Accidents of Note as Hath Hapned in Virginia …* of 1608. The visual details in the riddle are inspired by the scene in the engraved version of the map of Virginia by William Hole.

Like many of the stories on which the riddles in this book are based, it's become the stuff of legend. But did it really happen?

Thomas Fuller, writing in 1662, seems to have doubted it. In his *Worthies of England* of 1662, he wrote, 'it soundeth much to the diminution of [Captain Smith's] deeds that he alone is the herauld to proclaim them'.

Smith's later book, *The True Travels, Adventures, and Observations …*, first published in 1630, covers his earlier swash-buckling adventures in detail, but refers the reader to the *Genrall Historie* for an account of his experiences in Virginia. His *Advertisements for the Unexperienced Planters of New England, or Any Where* of 1631 presents a far more practical collection of hints and tips on how a colony could survive in the harsh conditions of the New World, and how it could, in his view, flourish.

The event happened around 1608. Pocahontas died in 1617. Her father died a year later. John Rolfe, whom Pocahontas married in 1614, died in 1622. It may have been out of respect for them that John Smith deliberately withheld the publication of his story until after their deaths. This could explain why Smith, who had many stories to tell, and good reasons to tell them, delayed writing about this particular one. It could also be that he asked others not to share it either. If nothing else, the argument casts reasonable doubt on the view that the story is necessarily false just because John Smith himself told it and waited until 1624 before publishing it.

Explore further

The prevailing views of the validity of the 'Cap'n Smith and Pocohantas' story are ably summarised by the American scholar, Michelle LeMaster in her survey of accounts of Pocahontas's biographies (A30) and Alden Vaughan's *New York Times* review (A49) of Barbour's *The Complete Works of Captain John Smith* (B8).

The story's caught the public's imagination, and has been retold over the years in many ways, most recently in film, with Disney's *Pocahontas* (1995) and Terrence Malick's *The New World* (2005).

The story presented here is just one episode in Captain Smith's life. A compelling account of his exploits, and the role he played in the larger context of the expansion of the British Empire and the development of the Commonwealth of Nations, is presented by H Wood Jarvis in *The Forgotten Adventure* (B55). Hole's *Map of Virginia* is viewable on the Wikimedia website (C36)

Why not do some additional research around John Smith and the early days of the colony in Virginia? I recommend two collections of primary sources – Barbour's, referenced above (B8), and Edward Haile's *Jamestown Narratives* (B41).

Terrible Twos

Judea, 2 years after the birth of Jesus—King Herod orders the execution of all male children under the age of 2 in and around Bethlehem.

This riddle covers the story related in the Gospel of Matthew (2:16–18) which has become known as 'The Massacre of the Innocents'. It is a widely accepted story that has been told in many ways, at different times. It has been included in Mystery Plays, and collections of stories from the Bible. It has inspired works of art and literature. However, it raises several questions, the main one being, 'Did it ever happen?'

One argument against it having happened is that the commonly accepted dates for Herod's death and Jesus' birth just don't coincide. According to some, Herod died in 4 BCE. According to others, he lived to 1 BCE. Either way, there's a 3- to 6-year gap in the accepted chronology. Another argument is that it neither features in the Gnostic Gospels, or in Josephus' *Antiquities of the Jews*. The story does appear, however, in *The Gospel of Pseudo-Matthew* (16–17), and the infancy gospel known as *The Arabic Gospel of the Infancy of the Saviour* (9–11).

On the flip side, the German Coptologist, Otto Meinardus, argues that the commonly accepted date of Jesus' birth, on which the commonly used BCE/CE dating system is based is incorrect. It was established in the sixth century by a monk called Dionysius Exiguus (also known as Dennis the Dwarf) as an improvement on the other dating systems in use at the time. It provided Christians with a dating system they could rely on to set the date of Easter. It also helped reconcile apocalyptic beliefs with a dating system that moved the supposed date of the end of the world further into the future. By the eighth century, Dennis the Dwarf's dating system had replaced that of the Roman Empire, which calculated its yearly cycles from the time of the foundation of Rome (AUC: *ab urbe condita*), and the Alexandrian systems, one of which took its starting point from the era of the last great persecution of Christians by the Emperor Diocletian (AM: *anno martyrum*), and the other from the supposed creation of the world (also AM – in this case, *anno mundi*). Meinardus puts forward the theory that Dionysius' dating was out by about 4 years, which explains the discrepancy in dates between the event of Jesus's birth, and Herod's reported actions within a couple of years of that.

The other major question the story raises is to do with exactly how many children died. Those who died in the massacre are considered martyrs by the Church, and are remembered in the Orthodox Church calendar on 29 December, observed as the Feast of the 14,000 Innocents. According to Trench, the number is a link with the 144,000 beings mentioned in Revelations (14:1) downsized by a sceptical cleric either in a moment of doubt, or more likely, in my view, due to the omission of a single digit somewhere along the way. He and other scholars argue, while acknowledging the horrific nature of the event, that the scale of the massacre may not have been as dramatic quantitatively as people might imagine, based on estimates of the population at the time.

The rather gruesome wording in this riddle is based on reported historical practice in a paper by Mans on early retellings of the story in the works of the early Church Fathers. It should be noted that in the fifth century, Macrobius wrote a differing account of the story:

> When it was heard that, as part of the slaughter of boys up to two years old, Herod, king of the Jews, had ordered his own son to be killed, he [the Emperor Augustus] remarked, "It is better to be Herod's pig [Greek: hys] than his son" [Greek: huios].

Explore further

Oscar Wilde, as quoted at the beginning of the introduction to this book, said the one duty we owe to history is to rewrite it. If you were to take on that duty in relation to this story, how would *you* choose to depict the scene?

In looking at others' accounts of the story while researching this riddle, I was struck by the emphasis on the wording in some of the children's books which feature stories from the Bible – for instance, Bishop John Vincent's in *My Mother's Bible Stories, Told in the Language of a Gentle Loving Mother Conversing with her Children* (B134 – pp 315–317), which ends, completely at odds with the title of the book, with this sentence: 'The cruel king died of a frightful disease soon after this murder of the innocent babes, and the worms ate his body.' Elsa Barker's and Peter Parley's versions are far gentler by comparison (B9 – p 38 and B88 – p 162 respectively).

Macrobius' account comes from his *Saturnalia* (C49 – Book 2, Section 4, Line 11). The Arabic Gospel of the Infancy of the Saviour and the gnostic gospel of Pseudo-Matthew, both of which include the story of the Massacre of the Innocents, are accessible on the New Advent and Gnostic Society Library websites (B2 and B99 respectively). An account of how the figure of Herod and the story of the Massacre were treated in English Mystery Plays, see Rosemary Woolf's work on *The English Mystery Plays* (B148 – pp 202–207).

For Otto Meinardus's views on the dating of the birth of Jesus, see the section in Chapter 2 of his book, *Two Thousand Years of Coptic Christianity* (A35 – p 14). For views on the number of children killed, see Richard Trench's *The Star of the Wise Men* (B128 – pp 102–104), Frederick Holweck's article on the *Holy Innocents* in *The Catholic Encyclopedia* (A21), Gordon Franz's article, *The Slaughter of the Innocents* (A15) and Prof Dr MK Mans' article on *The early Latin Church Fathers on Herod and the Infanticide* (A33).

Words are not the only medium through which this story has been told. The painting by Pieter Bruegel the Elder (C17) inspired a moving literary response from the Dutch playwright and novelist Maurice Maeterlinck (B69). Other artistic depictions, which could spark off several research studies in themselves, include works by Guido Reni (C64) and Peter Paul Rubens (C65 and C66), among others.

Time!

Plymouth Hoe, Plymouth, England, 1588—Sir Francis Drake finishes a game of bowls before taking to sea to engage the Spanish Armada in battle. It's a good story, which has come down through the years as a legend, but is it true? The first written account comes from Stow's *Annals* for 1600, although Drake isn't named in it. The account goes that 'officers and others kept revels on the shore, dancing, bowling, and making merry … at the instant of the foe's approach.' In Thomas Scott's pamphlet, *Second Part of Vox Populi* of 1624, there's a similar account of 'Commanders and Captaines … at bowles upon the hoe of Plimouth'. Again, Drake's name isn't mentioned. While some historians dismiss the story as the stuff of later legend (like many others linked to Drake's name), arguing that – for one thing – 'bowling on public ground was forbidden at that time', others (whose view I lean towards) accept the persistence of the legend in oral history, while maintaining an open mind as to how much of this was propaganda and how much based on fact. They argue, in support of their interpretation, that the tide would not have been flowing in his favour at the time, necessitating a delay in setting sail.

There are two replicas of the *Golden Hinde*, the ship in which Drake circumnavigated the world – one at Brixham Harbour, the other in London, moored near Southwark Cathedral.

Explore further

You can find out more about Sir Francis Drake in John Cummins' *Francis Drake: The Lives of a Hero* (B27) and Harry Kelsey's *Sir Francis Drake: The Queen's Pirate* (B57) as well as the latter's article on Drake in the *Oxford Dictionary of National Biography* (A26).

An overview of this and other legends associated with Drake can be found in Susan Jackson's article about *Drake Legends* on the Drake Exploration Society website (A22).

Hans Kraus's *Sir Francis Drake: A Pictorial Biography* which includes a particularly rich collection of primary sources relating to Drake's voyages is available on line on the Library of Congress website (B61).

The reference to Drake singeing the King of Spain's beard comes from Francis Bacon's *Considerations Touching a Warre with Spaine* (B6 – p 309).

Torches

Rome, 65 CE—The Emperor Nero decrees that the philosopher Seneca, his old tutor, should commit suicide.

We're in a smart, but tasteful villa on the outskirts of Rome. The hosts are entertaining the philosopher Seneca and his wife, Pompeia Paulina, during the notorious reign of the emperor Nero. Seneca is talking to them about the latest additions he's made to the book he's writing – his thoughts on how earthquakes come about, how rainbows are formed, how thunder and lightning occur … when a slave enters to say the house is surrounded by a troop of soldiers. A tribune enters to accuse Seneca of being involved in a plot orchestrated by the orator and statesman, Gaius Calpurnius Piso, who wanted to overthrow Nero and become emperor. The plot failed and Seneca was ordered to commit suicide along with all those implicated. Most writers believe that Seneca was unlikely to have been involved, and that this was just one of Nero's moves to get rid of people who annoyed him for whatever reason.

Seneca was a stoic philosopher, like Socrates before him and, like Socrates, looked on the act of dying in neutral terms. Both committed suicide when ordered to. As Epicurus later stated, in his *Letter to Menoeceus*,

> … many [people] at one moment shun death as the greatest of evils, at another (yearn for it) as a respite from the (evils) in life. (But the wise man neither seeks to escape life) nor fears the cessation of life, for neither does life offend him nor does the absence of life seem to be any evil.

The poem quoted in full at the end of the riddle is a sonnet called *The Death of Seneca* by the British poet, Mike Ellwood, reproduced here with his kind permission.

Explore further

This account of Seneca's life is based on Suetonius' *Life of Nero* (B121 – Book 6 – Volume 2, pp 85–188); Eutropius' *Roman History* (B35 – Book 7, Chapters 14/15 – pp 52/53) and Tacitus' account of Nero's life (B122 – Book 3, Chapters 29 ff – pp 83 ff). Many aspects of his life have been left out of this account, which focuses on the relationship between Nero and Seneca. Some contemporary scholars side with Tacitus and claim Nero didn't intend to commit arson and set fire to Rome. After all, his own palace was destroyed in the fire. Others side with Suetonius and Dio and argue that he was perfectly capable of it. A balanced reading of both types of sources is advised.

Edward Champlin's *Nero* is a particularly good book which covers the main issues, as well as some of the material omitted in this overview of his life (B20). Mary Francis Gyles' informed discussion of how the phrase, 'Nero fiddled while Rome burned' came about, with a critical examination of the relevant primary and secondary sources, is also worth reading (A18).

The full text of Epicurus' letter can be found in Cyril Bailey's edition of his extant works (B34 – pp 82–93).

Travellers' Tales

The dining room at the Polos' house, Venice, 1295—Marco Polo tells of his travels to and from China.

The two main questions raised by this riddle are: (1) Is the story of Marco's jewel-sharing real? and (2) Can his account of his journeys be believed?

Regarding the first question, the story of Marco distributing hidden jewels at his dinner party was first put into writing by Ramusio, whose biography of Marco Polo appeared in the second (and the only posthumously published) volume of his 3-volume work, *Navigationi e Viaggi* – a collection of the lives and expeditions of various travellers and explorers, printed in 1559. According to the account in the book, Ramusio had heard this particular story in person from an elderly senator of his time, Gasparo Malpiero, whose family house was near the Polos', and who, in turn, had heard the story from both his father and his grandfather. It was also told among his neighbours. From there, the legend spread.

Ramusio's version of the story appears in an English translation by Henry Yule in the Introductory Notices to his 1871 translation of Marco Polo's book thus:

> And when they got thither [to Venice] the same fate befel them as befel Ulysses, who, when he returned, after his twenty years' wanderings, to his native Ithaca, was recognized by nobody. Thus also those three gentlemen who had been so many years absent from their native city were recognized by none of their kinsfolk, who were under the firm belief that they had all been dead for many a year past, as indeed had been reported. Through the long duration and the hardships of their journeys, and through the many worries and anxieties that they had undergone, they were quite changed in aspect, and had got a certain indescribable smack of the Tartar both in air and accent, having indeed all but forgotten their Venetian tongue. Their clothes too were coarse and shabby, and of a Tartar cut. They proceeded on their arrival to their house in this city in the confine of St. John Chrysostom, where you may see it to this day. The house, which was in those days a very lofty and handsome palazzo, is now known by the name of the Corte del Millioni for a reason that I will tell you presently. Going thither they found it occupied by some of their relatives, and they had the greatest difficulty in making the latter understand who they should be. For these good people,

seeing them to be in countenance so unlike what they used to be, and in dress so shabby, flatly refused to believe that they were those very gentlemen of the Ca' Polo whom they had been looking upon for ever so many years as among the dead. So these three gentlemen,— this is a story I have often heard when I was a youngster from the illustrious Messer GASPARO MALPIERO, a gentleman of very great age, and a Senator of eminent virtue and integrity, whose house was on the Canal of Santa Marina, exactly at the corner over the mouth of the Rio di S. Giovanni Chrisostomo, and just midway among the buildings of the aforesaid Corte del Millioni, and he said he had heard the story from his own father and grandfather, and from other old men among the neighbours,— the three gentlemen, I say, devised a scheme by which they should at once bring about their recognition by their relatives, and secure the honourable notice of the whole city; and this was it:—

They invited a number of their kindred to an entertainment, which they took care to have prepared with great state and splendour in that house of theirs; and when the hour arrived for sitting down to table they came forth of their chamber all three clothed in crimson satin, fashioned in long robes reaching to the ground such as people in those days wore within doors. And when water for the hands had been served, and the guests were set, they took off those robes and put on others of crimson damask, whilst the first suits were by their orders cut up and divided among the servants. Then after partaking of some of the dishes they went out again and came back in robes of crimson velvet, and when they had again taken their seats, the second suits were divided as before. When dinner was over they did the like with the robes of velvet, after they had put on dresses of the ordinary fashion worn by the rest of the company. These proceedings caused much wonder and amazement among the guests. But when the cloth had been drawn, and all the servants had been ordered to retire from the dining hall, Messer Marco, as the youngest of the three, rose from table, and, going into another chamber, brought forth the three shabby dresses of coarse stuff which they had worn when they first arrived. Straightway they took sharp knives and began to rip up some of the seams and welts, and to take out of them jewels of the greatest value in vast quantities, such as rubies, sapphires, carbuncles, diamonds and emeralds, which had all been stitched up in those dresses in so artful a fashion that nobody could have suspected the fact. For when they took leave of the Great Can they had changed all the wealth that he had bestowed upon them into this mass of rubies, emeralds, and other jewels, being well aware of the impossibility of carrying with them so great an amount in gold over a journey of such extreme length and difficulty. Now this exhibition of such a huge treasure of jewels and precious stones, all tumbled out upon the table, threw the guests into fresh amazement, insomuch that they seemed quite bewildered and dumbfounded. And now they recognized that in spite of all former doubts these were in truth those honoured and worthy gentlemen of the Ca' Polo that they claimed to be; and so all paid them the greatest honour and reverence. And when the story got wind in Venice, straightway the whole city, gentle and simple, flocked to the house to embrace them, and to make much of them, with every conceivable demonstration of affection and respect. On Messer Maffio, who was the eldest, they conferred the honours of an office that was of great dignity in those days; whilst the young men came daily to visit and converse with the ever polite and gracious Messer Marco, and to ask him questions about Cathay and the Great Can, all which he answered with such kindly courtesy that every man felt himself in a manner his debtor. And as it happened that in the story, which he was constantly called on

> to repeat, of the magnificence of the Great Can, he would speak of his revenues as amounting to ten or fifteen millions of gold; and in like manner, when recounting other instances of great wealth in those parts, would always make use of the term millions, so they gave him the nickname of MESSER MARCO MILLIONI: a thing which I have noted also in the Public Books of this Republic where mention is made of him.

Ramusio states that the oral accounts of the story arose in the same geographical quarter as the event was supposed to have happened. However, the house in which the party was held could only have been the Palazzo di San Felice, the Polos' house at the time, which was in a different area. It was after the merchants' return from their travels that the family moved to the Ca' Polo, on the Rio di S. Giovanni Chrisostomo which they had built (or more likely modified) at some point between their return in 1295 and the drawing up of Maffeo Polo's will in 1300, in which it is first mentioned – as far as we currently know – as the Polos' residence. It could be that the scene took place here, after they moved, although the story itself indicates that it happened shortly after their return; or that the story continued to circulate and was told in the quarter to which they moved. I leave the balance of credibility and entertainment value to individual readers to determine for themselves.

A variation of the story appears in Marco Barbaro's account of Marco Polo's life, written in 1536, nearly 250 years after the event, but published before Ramusio's. In it, the wife of one of the merchants gives his shabby clothes to a beggar, not knowing he's hidden jewels in it. He regains the garment by standing on the Rialto Bridge constantly turning a wheel, thereby attracting the attention of passers-by, spreading the news of an unusual event, thereby drawing more curious viewers to him including, finally, the person wearing the garment, which he manages to recover by negotiating a mutually agreeable exchange.

Factors such as the lapse of time between this alleged event and the appearance of this story in print, as well as the likely weight of the garment, raise questions about its authenticity. Even if there were just a small number of small jewels, wouldn't the new owner have noticed? Most telling, however, is the fact that the person who gives the garment away in the story is portrayed as one of the travellers' wives. Marco was unmarried at the time; his mother, Niccolò's wife, had died while they were away, leaving only the possibility of the woman being Maffeo's wife. While Yule's genealogy makes no mention of Maffeo being married, Moule and Pelliot's later version shows him as being married, although no date is given for the marriage, which presumably took place after their return. It is a point that casts doubt upon the veracity of this particular version of the tale, at least.

Perhaps Malpiero's version was an attempt to set the record straight. It's a moot point.

So much for the question of the veracity of the 'jewel' story. Regarding the second question, while in recent times scholars such as Frances Wood have started to question the veracity of Marco's account, his account has a long history of being called into question. Following his return, Marco quickly became labelled as a teller of tall tales, a lover of exaggeration, whose favourite word, apparently, was 'millions', with the Tuscan version of his book being called *Il Milione* (The Million). For years after his book appeared, the figure of Marco of the Millions featured as a comedic stock character in *Commedia dell'Arte* performances.

However, while people in the fourteenth to sixteenth centuries had only incredulity and a comparatively limited world view to base their mockery on, modern scholars choose to question his stories on the basis of different logical premises, their main arguments being that there's no mention of Marco Polo in Chinese accounts of the time, nor is there any mention of the

Great Wall, or customs such as foot-binding in his account. They conclude, therefore, that it's possible that much of Marco's account was hearsay rather than directly witnessed. Counter-arguments have been put forward by others such as Arthur N Waldron, Luce Boulnois, Francis Woodman Cleaves, Hans Ulrich Vogel, and Igor de Rachewiltz who find Marco's account credible, while still interpreting it critically.

Explore further

The primary sources for the story on which this riddle is based are Ramusio's *Navigationi et Viaggi* (B101), and the translations of Marco Polo's book by Yule (B95) and Moule and Pelliot (B96). The main arguments against Marco Polo ever having been to China are put forward in Frances Wood's book *Did Marco Polo Go to China?* (B147). If you want to explore the counter-arguments further, see Arthur Waldron's article, *The Problem of the Great Wall of China* (A50), Luce Boulnois's book, *Silk Road* (B14), Francis Cleaves' article, *A Chinese Source Bearing on Marco Polo's Departure from China and a Persian Source on His Arrival in Persia* (A8), Hans Vogel's book, *Marco Polo Was in China: New Evidence from Currencies, Salts and Revenues* (B136) and Igor de Rachewiltz's paper, *Marco Polo Went to China* (A10).

A particularly good overview of both the history of the dissemination of Marco's book and the arguments relating to the veracity of his account can be found in Haw's *Marco Polo's China: A Venetian in the Realm of Khubilai Khan* (B44).

Marco Polo's account had considerable influence on future generations. Columbus is known to have taken a copy of Marco's book with him in 1492 when he 'sailed the ocean blue'. Coleridge found inspiration in Samuel Purchas's retelling of scenes from Polo's book which led to his classic poem *Kubla Khan, or A Vision in a Dream. A Fragment*. And the Italian author, Italo Calvino, explored the relationship between Kublai Khan and Marco Polo, Marco's storytelling skills and the liminal worlds of imagined recreations of the complex wholes that make up the ever-changing characters of cities in his *Invisible Cities* (B17).

An extremely readable account for young readers, which is faithful to Marco's original sources, is Louise Andrews Kent's book, *He Went With Marco Polo* (B58), which I myself enjoyed reading very much as a child.

Vision

A Native American tribal gathering near the Little Bighorn River, Black Hill Country, North America, sometime between 17 and 25 June 1876—Sitting Bull relates his Sun Dance vision to members of the gathered tribes between The Battle of the Rosebud and The Battle of the Little Bighorn.

This event describes an episode in American history in which members of the Sioux nation (made up of Santee, Yankton and Lakota tribes) met to perform a ritual Sun Dance. During this event, Sitting Bull, a Lakota warrior chief who was around 45 years old at the time, sought to engage in a vision quest that would help the native tribes withstand the increasing pressure from the invading settlers to limit their territory and take over their land.

It was not the first time that Sitting Bull had engaged in a vision quest. Previous instances had occurred in 1870, prior to an attack against the Flatheads, when he had a vision of a ball of fire coming towards him, which later turned out to be a rifle shot which hit his arm; and during the Sun Dance meeting in 1875, the year before The Battle of the Little Bighorn, when it was revealed to him that the tribes would face war. It was not clear at that point whether they would be fighting against each other, or against the US army. It was only after a night raid by the US army on a Native American camp by the Powder River on 17 March 1876 that it became clear that the US army was on the warpath. The army had instructions to uphold a decree to limit Native Americans to a designated reservation by force.

Many Native Americans, under the leadership of Red Cloud,

had agreed to live on the Great Sioux Reservation under the terms of the treaty drawn up in 1868. Sitting Bull, who was a signatory to it, was among them. Later he, Crazy Horse of the Oglalas, and their followers resolved to defend their way of life through force of arms, following incursions by the US army, and the increasing pressure on their territory as a result of the California gold rush, which prompted the US Government to attempt to buy Black Hill land from the Indians – a move which Sitting Bull and Crazy Horse were resolved to resist.

Both sides were prepared for conflict. The US army pressed forwards. The Native Americans stood their ground, joining forces under Sitting Bull's leadership. The army attacked a Cheyenne camp at the Battle of Powder River in the early hours of the freezing cold morning of 16 March 1876, burning their goods and supplies and capturing their horses. The Cheyenne later regained most of these, and retreated to Crazy Horse's encampment, from where they travelled on to join Sitting Bull.

In June 1876, the US army launched a three-pronged attack aiming to force the Native Americans to retreat to their reservation. The force which advanced from the north, led by General Crook contained not only 'Calamity Jane' but also Frank Grouard, who was then acting as a scout and interpreter to General Cook. Grouard was a man of mixed race origin, who worked as a mail carrier and stagecoach driver. On one of his trips, he had been attacked by Crow Indians who took everything he had and abandoned him in a nearby forest, where he was found by members of a Sioux band who rescued him. He was eventually accepted into the tribe and adopted by Sitting Bull as a brother. He later left the tribe and ended up playing a key role in the negotiation of treaties between the Native Americans and the whites.

It was thanks to Grouard that the army band had found their way to the Native American camp at Powder River and Sitting Bull wanted revenge. The armies engaged for the best part of the day, then retreated, with no clear winner. Although the US army had control of the battlefield, they swiftly retreated from it to their camp.

The Native Americans regrouped and held a Sun Dance. It was during this dance that Sitting Bull had his famous vision which predicted victory for the Native Americans in an upcoming battle. This was, indeed, the outcome of The Battle of The Little Bighorn, which has also gone down in history as Custer's Last Stand. While the Native Americans won the battle, they ultimately lost the war. Sitting Bull was forced to retreat to Canada with many of his surviving companions and the US Government eventually regained the territory they wished to reclaim, in return for taking on the responsibility of supplying the Native Americans within the reservations with rations.

The terms of exchange continue to be challenged by the Native Americans. In 1980, the outcome of the Supreme Court case *United States v. Sioux Nation of Indians* found in favour of the Sioux. The compensation offered, however, was unacceptable to the Sioux, who continue to claim their right to the land.

Explore further

For more information on Sitting Bull, see historian Robert Utley's book, *The Lance and the Shield: The Life and Times of Sitting Bull* (B132) and the book by Sitting Bull's great grandson, Ernie LaPointe, *Sitting Bull: His Life and Legacy* (B62).

More information on the Battle of the Little Big Horn and the people involved in it can be found in Nathaniel Philbrick's *The Last Stand* (B90), James McLaird's *Calamity Jane* (B77) and Joe de Barthe's *The Life and Adventures of Frank Grouard* (B30).

Facsimiles of the original 1868 treaty document can be viewed on line on the US National Archives and Records Administration website (C20). The US Supreme Court records of the 1980 court case between the United States and the Sioux Nation can be accessed on the Justia website (C81).

Webs

Abbotsford, Scotland, 1827—Sir Walter Scott in his study, writing his version of the story of King Bruce and the spider.

Sir Walter Scott in this scene is 55 years old. One of the most popular writers of his age, a contemporary of Jane Austen and one of her early admirers, he started out as a sickly child in Edinburgh, who suffered from polio, which left him with a permanent limp. To recover from the disease, he was sent to live with his grandparents and his paternal aunt, who lived on a farm in the Scottish borders. She taught him to read, and was an early influence on his literary development and his love of stories. Although he graduated in law, his first love was poetry. In his late twenties and early thirties, he would go out and collect ballads and stories that people sang and told, which proved popular when they were published. He followed these with what is widely believed to be the first historical novel in English, an account of how Edward Waverley, an Englishman, travels up from the South of England through Scotland, and gets caught up in the 1745 Jacobite uprising. Worried that his reputation as a poet would be diminished by having his name associated with this work, he published it anonymously, a decision he stuck with for the remaining 19 books in the series known as the *Waverley Novels*.

In 1818, he led a campaign to recover the Honours of Scotland, Scotland's coronation regalia, which had been locked away since 1707, when England and Scotland had been united under the name of Great Britain as a result of the *Treaty of Union*.

Scott was a highly successful writer. However, he'd invested in printing and publishing – not always sensibly. He'd taken out loans to finance his building projects, and accepted advances on works he hadn't completed. The financial crash of 1825 hit all the investors badly, leaving them exposed financially and Scott liable for debts of £126,000 (more than £10 m in 2014 terms, according to the Abbotsford website). He liquidated available assets and, refusing to accept loans from supporters (who included King George IV), with the agreement of his creditors and bankers, set up a trust into which all rights to his published works would be paid. When it came to paying off his debts, "my own right hand shall do it," was what he said. While he suffered a mild stroke in 1826, he kept his word and worked hard to generate enough earnings to keep his creditors satisfied.

At this point, Scott was finishing his *Life of Napoleon*. An entry for 24 May 1827 in Scott's journal – a journal which he started keeping in 1825, as a result of reading the first published edition of Samuel Pepys's diary which had just come out, and some of Byron's notes on it – reads,

> A good thought came into my head: to write stories for little Johnnie Lockhart from the History of Scotland, like those taken from the History of England. I will not write mine quite so simply as Croker has done. I am persuaded both children and the lower class of readers hate books which are written down to their capacity, and love those that are more composed for their elders and betters. I will make, if possible, a book that a child will understand, yet a man will feel some temptation to peruse should he chance to take it up. It will require, however, a simplicity of style not quite my own. The grand and interesting consists in ideas, not in words.

The collection of stories from Scottish history first came out in 1827, with a dedication to his then 6-year old grandchild John Hugh Lockhart, a sickly child nicknamed Hugh Littlejohn, Esq, for whom I would imagine Scott had particular empathy, having suffered from long-term childhood illness himself.

The story which forms the subject of this riddle is contained within Scott's account of *King Robert the Bruce*. The story continues with the king thinking,

> "as I have no means of knowing what is best to be done, I will be guided by the luck which shall attend this spider. If the insect shall make another attempt to fix its thread, and shall be successful, I will venture a seventh time to try my fortune in Scotland; but if the spider shall fail I will go to the wars in Palestine, and never return to my native country more."
>
> While Bruce was forming this resolution, the spider made another exertion with all the force it could muster, and fairly succeeded in fastening its thread to the beam which it had so often in vain attempted to reach. Bruce, seeing the success of the spider, resolved to try his own fortune; and as he had never before gained a victory, so he never afterwards sustained any considerable or decisive check or defeat. I have often met with people of the name of Bruce, so completely persuaded of the truth of this story, that they would not on any account kill a spider; because it was that insect which had shown the example of perseverance, and given a signal of good luck to their great namesake.

King Robert the Bruce succeeded in fighting off the English and regaining Scottish sovereignty and independence. After he died, at his request, his embalmed heart was taken on a crusade by James Douglas, his best friend, who joined King Alfonso XI's campaign to reclaim the Holy Land. Douglas never made it to Jerusalem. He died in battle at Teba in 1330, but Robert's heart was recovered and taken back to Scotland. It was ceremoniously buried beneath the high altar at Melrose Abbey, Scotland, where it remains to this day.

Explore further

The story of *King Bruce and the Spider* first passed into print with Scott's account. Where the story came from is unclear, although it would seem to be a story Scott knew from an oral tradition, as he is known to have actively collected such stories. There is a similar story in David Hume's account of 'Sir James "The Black" Douglas' in *The History of the House and Race of Douglas*, published posthumously in 1643, and added to Hume's manuscript by his daughter (A42, B50). Hume's has the spider trying to climb up its web, to the height of a tree, but the web collapsing. The spider only manages to attain the height it is aiming for on the twelfth attempt. Later versions of the story have King Bruce in a cave, following either local legends or wishful thinking.

The story also appears in the *Mirâdj-nâmeh*, a Turkish illuminated manuscript of the fifteenth century which includes accounts of Mohammed's ascension to heaven and the life of Tamburlaine (also known as Tamerlane or Timur) (C25 – pp 71/2). It is in the latter story that the story appears, although in this version, the wounded Tamburlaine watches an ant climbing and slipping down a wall seven times before finally successfully reaching the top on the eighth. Unlike Scott's version, both the other accounts are set outdoors.

You can find out more about Sir Walter Scott in his own account of his life, published in 1831 (B115) and his diaries, which were edited and published in 1891 by David Douglas (B32). Numerous biographies are available. The 10-volume work by John Gibson Lockhart, Scott's son-in-law, published in 1837 (B65) heads up the collection, which includes a notable biography by John Buchan (B15). Further information can be found on the Walter Scott Digital Archive website, hosted by the University of Edinburgh (C75).

More about Abbotsford can be found on the Abbotsford website (A3) and in Leslie Stephen's *The Story of Scott's Ruin* (A45).

Many of Scott's works have inspired films. Ivanhoe, for one, has inspired several, while Scott's *The Bride of Lammermoor* was the inspiration for Donizetti and Cammarano's opera, *Lucia di Lammermoor*. The story of Robert the Bruce has been freely retold for cinema in *Braveheart* (1995), which features Mel Gibson (who also directed the film) as Robert. An animated interpretation of the story of King Bruce and the Spider appears (along with the story of Columbus) in a song called *Stick-to-it-ivity* in the 1948 Disney film *So Dear to My Heart*. In this retelling, the scene takes place in the open air.

Indices

Riddles in chronological order

	Riddle	Clues	Key
KKM	9	36	87
Hoopoe	14	35	83
Elephants	23	35	78
15	21	32	43
Asp	5	32	49
Terrible Twos	13	39	127
Shells	8	38	112
Revolt	22	37	101
Torches	28	40	132
Pine Tree	4	37	98
Cinders	25	34	74
Sealed	5	38	105
Travellers' Tales	24	40	133
Webs (Core story)	27	41	143
Bonfire	18	34	70
G	4	35	81
Maps	12	36	94
Bang!	3	32	52
Time!	7	40	131
Blast!	10	33	61
Stop!	16	39	126
Bones	13	33	65
Stars	11	39	123
Revolution	6	37	103
Bees	15	33	57
Webs (Frame story)	27	41	143
Vision	3	41	140
A photo shoot?!	7	32	45
Never Man	10	37	95

Stand up!	17	38	116
Life and death	19	36	89

Riddles in alphabetical order

	Riddle	Clues	Key
15	20	32	43
A photo shoot?!	7	32	45
Asp	5	32	49
Bang!	3	32	52
Bees	15	33	57
Blast!	9	33	61
Bones	12	33	65
Bonfire	18	34	70
Cinders	25	34	74
Elephants	23	35	78
G	4	35	81
Hoopoe	14	35	83
KKM	9	36	87
Life and death	19	36	89
Maps	12	36	94
Never Man	10	37	95
Pine Tree	4	37	98
Revolt	22	37	101
Revolution	6	37	103
Sealed	5	38	105
Shells	8	38	112
Stand up!	17	38	116
Stars	11	39	123
Stop!	16	39	126
Terrible Twos	13	39	127
Time!	7	40	131
Torches	28	40	132
Travellers' Tales	24	40	133
Vision	3	41	140
Webs (Core story)	27	41	143
Webs (Frame story)	27	41	143

Riddles grouped thematically

Justice-Injustice

15 20
A photo shoot?! 7
Blast! 9
Bones 12
Elephants 23
Life and death 19
Never Man 10
Revolution 6
Sealed 5
Stand up! 17
Stop! 16
Terrible Twos 13
Torches 28

Politics

15 20
A photo shoot?! 7
Bones 12
Bonfire 18
Elephants 23
Life and death 19
Maps 12
Never Man 10
Revolution 6
Sealed 5
Shells 8
Stars 11
Stop! 16
Terrible Twos 13
Time! 7
Torches 28

Vision	3
Webs	27

Ethics

15	20
A photo shoot?!	7
Life and death	19
Revolution	6
Sealed	5
Stand up!	17
Stop!	16
Terrible Twos	13
Time!	7
Torches	28
Vision	3
Webs	27

Human Greatness and Achievement

Asp	5
Bees	15
Bonfire	18
Cinders	25
Elephants	23
G	4
KKM	9
Life and death	19
Maps	12
Never Man	10
Revolt	22
Sealed	5
Stand up!	17
Stop!	16
Time!	7
Travellers' Tales	24

Vision	3
Webs	27

Law

15	20
A photo shoot?!	7
Bonfire	18
Life and death	19
Sealed	5
Stop!	16
Time!	7
Vision	3

Religion

Bang!	3
Blast!	9
Bones	12
KKM	9
Maps	12
Stop!	16
Terrible Twos	13
Time!	7
Vision	3

Wisdom

Hoopoe	14
Stop!	16
Torches	28
Travellers' Tales	24
Vision	3

Love

Asp	5
Stop!	16

Other

Pine Tree 4
Revolt 22
Revolution 6
Sealed 5
Shells 8
Stars 11
Stop! 16
Time! 7
Travellers' Tales 24
Webs 27

Bibliography

Articles

A1 *A Russian Sect Canonizes Nicholas II*, in *The New York Times*, 2 November 1981; *The New York Times* website, date as stated, http://www.nytimes.com/1981/11/02/nyregion/a-russian-sect-canonizes-nicholas-ii.html.

A2 Anon, *Ft. Dix Wac asks $25,000 In Jim Crow Bus Suit*, in *Jet*, 24 September 1953, Chicago, IL: Johnson Publishing Company, p 6. http://books.google.co.uk/books?id=t0IDAAAAMBAJ&pg=PA6.

A3 Anon, *Visitor Centre: Exhibition*, Abbotsford website, no date, http://www.scottsabbotsford.com/visit/visitor-centre.

A4 Barry, M, *Jamshêd and Solomon, The Solar Bird and Persian Civilization: Worldview and Timeline of 'Attâr's Canticle of the Birds*, in 'Attâr, F, *The Canticle of the Birds*, translated by Darbandi, A and Davis, D, Paris: Diane de Selliers, 2013, pp 419–430.

A5 Burdman, M, *New British Research Exposes Churchill as Genocidal Racist*, in *Executive Intelligence Review*, Volume 21, Number 21, 20 May 1994, pp 40–43.

A6 Canby, W, *The History of the Flag of the United States: A Paper Read before the Historical Society of Pennsylvania (March 1870)*, transcribed by Harker, JB, in the Betsy Ross Homepage section of the US history.org website, August 1999, http://www.ushistory.org/betsy/more/canby.htm.

A7 Cavendish, R, *'Bloody Sunday' in St Petersburg*, in *History Today*, Volume 55, Issue 1, 2005, *History Today* website, no date, http://www.historytoday.com/richard-cavendish/%E2%80%98bloody-sunday%E2%80%99-st-petersburg.

A8 Cleaves, FW, *A Chinese Source Bearing on Marco Polo's*

Departure from China and a Persian Source on His Arrival in Persia, in *Harvard Journal of Asiatic Studies*, Volume 36, 1976, pp 181–203.

A9 D, S, *Printing*, in *The Encyclopaedia Britannica: or Dictionary of Arts, Sciences, and General Literature*, 7th edition, 21 Volumes, Volume 18, pp 537–573; Google Books, no date, http://books.google.co.uk/books?id=ej87AQAAMAAJ&pg=PA542&lpg=PA542.

A10 de Rachewiltz, I, *Marco Polo Went to China*, in *Zentralasiatische Studien*, Volume 27, 1997, pp 34–92.

A11 Dunan, M, *La Taille de Napoléon*, in *Revue de l'Institut Napoléon*, Number 89, October 1963, pp 178–179, Fondation Napoléon website, no date, http://www.napoleon.org/fr/salle_lecture/articles/files/Taillenapo_RIN_89_oct1963_2006.asp.

A12 Elias, J, *Prophecy, Power and Propriety: The Encounter of Solomon and the Queen of Sheba*, in *Journal of Qur'anic Studies*, Volume XI, Issue 1, 2009, pp 57–74.

A13 Flavius Josephus, *Antiquities of the Jews*, in *The Works of Flavius Josephus*, translated by William Whiston, London: Ward, Lock & Co, Ltd, 1878.

A14 Flory, MB, *Pearls for Venus*, in *Historia: Zeitschrift für Alte Geschichte*, Volume 37, Number 4, Q4 1988, pp 498–504.

A15 Franz, G, *The Slaughter of the Innocents: Historical Fact or Legendary Fiction?*, Associates for Biblical Research website, 8 December 2009, http://www.biblearchaeology.org/post/2009/12/08/The-Slaughter-of-the-Innocents-Historical-Fact-or-Legendary-Fiction.aspx#Article.

A16 Godden, M, *The Old English Life of St Neot and the Legends of King Alfred*, in *Anglo-Saxon England*, Volume 39, 2010, pp 193–225.

A17 Grant, S, *Should We Ever Disobey the Law?*, in *Richmond Journal of Philosophy*, Volume 14 (Spring 2007).

A18 Gyles, MF, *Nero Fiddled While Rome Burned*, in *The Classical Journal*, Volume 42, Number 4 (January 1947), pp 211–217.

A19 Hannan, D, *Review of Pollard, J, Alfred the Great: the Man who Founded England*, in *The Telegraph*, 27 November 2005, *The Telegraph* website, http://www.telegraph.co.uk/culture/books/3648321/Alfred-the-Great-the-Man-who-Founded-England-by-Justin-Pollard-350pp-John-Murray-20-T-18-plus-1.25-pandp-0870-428-4112-The-only-great-king-of-England.html.

A20 Hartman, H, *Pardon Me? The Rosa Parks Act Sparks New Debate, The Huffington Post* website, Last updated 25 May 2011, http://www.huffingtonpost.com/hermene-hartman/pardon-me-the-rosa-parks_b_262614.html.

A21 Holweck, F, *Holy Innocents*, in *The Catholic Encyclopedia*, Volume 7, New York: Robert Appleton Company, 1910, New Advent website, 6 March 2014, http://www.newadvent.org/cathen/07419a.htm.

A22 Jackson, S, *Drake Legends*, The Drake Exploration Society website, no date, http://www.indrakeswake.co.uk/Society/Research/legends.htm.

A23 John I, *Concession of England to the Pope, 1213*, in Stubb's *Charters*, translated in Henderson, EF, *Select Historical Documents of the Middle Ages*, London: George Bell, 1910, pp 430–431, Fordham University Website, Medieval Sourcebook, 1996, http://www.fordham.edu/Halsall/source/john1a.asp.

A24 Judaeus, P [Philo], *A Treatise on the Virtues and on the Office of Ambassadors Addressed to Caius*, in *The Works of Philo Judaeus, the Contemporary of Josephus*, translated by Yonge, CD, London: Henry G. Bohn, 1855, 4 Volumes. Volume 4, pp 99–180, Chapters IV-XIV.

A25 Junghans, H, *Luther's Wittenberg*, translated by Gustavs, K, in *The Cambridge Companion to Martin Luther,* edited by McKim, DK, Cambridge: Cambridge University Press, 2003, pp 20–35.

A26 Kelsey, H, *Drake, Sir Francis* (1540–1596) in *Oxford Dictionary of National Biography,* Oxford University Press, 2004, Oxford Dictionary of National Biography website, May 2007, http://www.oxforddnb.com/templates/article.jsp?articleid=8022&back&version=2007-05.

A27 Kent, W, *Indulgences,* in *The Catholic Encyclopedia,* New York: Robert Appleton Company, 1910; New Advent website, 22 February 2014, http://www.newadvent.org/cathen/07783a.htm.

A28 Klein, HA, *Sacred Things and Holy Bodies: Collecting Relics from Late Antiquity to the Early Renaissance,* in *Treasures of Heaven: Saints, Relics, and Devotion in Medieval Europe* (Exhibition Catalogue), New Haven and London: Yale University Press, 2011, pp 55–68.

A29 Lehner, M, *Building an Old Kingdom Pyramid,* in *Pyramids: Treasures, Mysteries, and New Discoveries in Egypt,* edited by Hawass, Z, Vercelli: White Star Publishers, 2011, pp 46–59.

A30 LeMaster, M, *Pocahontas: (De)Constructing an American Myth,* in *The William and Mary Quarterly, Third Series,* Volume 62, Number 4 (October 2005), pp 774–781, JSTOR website, no date, http://www.jstor.org/stable/3491451.

A31 Levy, CJ, *The Georgian and Putin: A Hate Story, The New York Times Week in Review,* 18 April 2009; *The New York Times* website, date as stated, http://www.nytimes.com/2009/04/19/weekinreview/19levy.html.

A32 Mandela, N, *We Defy – 10,000 volunteers protest against unjust laws,* 30 August 1952, on the African National Congress (ANC) website, no date, http://www.anc.org.za/show.php?id=2592.

A33 Mans, MJ, *The early Latin Church Fathers on Herod and the Infanticide*, in *HTS Teologiese Studies/Theological Studies*, Volume 53, Numbers 1–2, 1997, Durbanville, South Africa: AOSIS Open Journals.

A34 McMenamin, M, *Depiction of the Alps on Punic coins from Campania, Italy*, in *Numismatics International Bulletin*, 2012, Volume 41 (1–2), pp 30–33.

A35 Meinardus, OFA, *The Birth of Christ*, in *Two Thousand Years of Coptic Christianity*, Cairo: The American University in Cairo Press, 1999, Chapter 2, p 14.

A36 Press Association, *Witchcraft Murder Couple Jailed for Life*, *The Guardian*, Monday, 5 March 2012, *The Guardian* website, date as stated, http://www.theguardian.com/uk/2012/mar/05/witchcraft-couple-jailed-for-life.

A37 Raffaele, P, *Keepers of the Lost Ark?*, in *Smithsonian Magazine*, December 2007, Smithsonian website, http://www.smithsonianmag.com/people-places/keepers-of-the-lost-ark-179998820/?c=y&page=1.

A38 Reisner, Professor GA, *Solving the History of the Sphinx*, in *Cosmopolitan Magazine*, Volume 53, 1929, pp 4–13.

A39 Rock, PMJ, *Canonical Age*, in *The Catholic Encyclopedia*, New York: Robert Appleton Company, 1907; New Advent website, 22 February 2014, www.newadvent.org/cathen/01206c.htm.

A40 Schechter, S, *The Riddles of Solomon in Rabbinic Literature*, in *Folk-Lore: A Quarterly Review of Myth, Tradition, Institution and Custom*, Volume 1, Number 3, pp 349–358.

A41 Schwartz, B, *Collective Forgetting and the Symbolic Power of Oneness: The Strange Apotheosis of Rosa Parks*, in *Social Psychology Quarterly*, Volume 72, Number 2 (June 2009), pp 123–142. 'Snap' version available at http://www.asanet.org/journals/spq/snaps.cfm#2009.

A42 Scott, WW, *Review of The History of the House of Douglas by*

David Hume of Godscroft, edited by David Reid, in *The Scottish Historical Review,* Volume 77, Number 204, Part 2, October 1998, pp 261–263, JSTOR website, no date, http://www.jstor.org/stable/25530844.

A43 Shaw, J, *Who Built the Pyramids,* in *The Harvard Magazine,* July–August 2003, pp 42–49, 99.

A44 Spaeth, JW, Jr., *Hannibal and Napoleon,* in *The Classical Journal,* Volume 24, Number 4 (January 1929), pp 291–293.

A45 Stephen, L, *The Story of Scott's Ruin,* in *Studies of a Biographer,* London: Duckworth & Co, 1898, 4 Volumes – Volume 2, pp 1–37. Wikisource website, http://en.wikisource.org/wiki/Studies_of_a_Biographer/The_Story_of_Scott%27s_Ruin.

A46 The Negro Ministers of Montgomery and Their Congregations, *To the Montgomery Public,* Advertisement in the *Alabama Journal,* 25 December 1955, Martin Luther King, Jr. and the Global Freedom Struggle website, facsimile and transcript, no date, http://mlk-kpp01.stanford.edu/index.php/encyclopedia/documentsentry/to_the_montgomery_public.

A47 Thompson, DJ, *Cleopatra VII: The Queen in Egypt,* in *Cleopatra Reassessed,* edited by Walker, S and Ashton, S-A, London: British Museum Press, 2003.

A48 Thoreau, HD, *Resistance to Civil Government,* in *Aesthetic Papers,* edited by Peabody, EP, Boston: The Editor, New York: G. P. Putnam, 1849, pp 189–213.

A49 Vaughan, A, *Beyond Pocahontas, Review of The Complete Works of Captain John Smith, edited by Barbour, PL, Chapel Hill: The Institute of Early American History and Culture/ The University of North Carolina Press, 1969–1979, 3 Volumes,* in *The New York Times,* 29 June 1986, *The New York Times* website, 1986, http://www.nytimes.com/1986/06/29/books/beyond-pocahontas.html?ref=bookreviews&pagewanted=1.

A50 Waldron, AN, *The Problem of the Great Wall of China*, in *Harvard Journal of Asiatic Studies*, Volume 43, Number 2, December 1983, pp 643–663.

A51 Woods, D, *Caligula's Seashells*, in *Greece & Rome*, Volume 47, Number 1, April 2000, pp 80–87.

A52 Yorke, B, *Alfred the Great: The Most Perfect Man in History?*, in *History Today*, Volume 49, Issue 10, 1999, *History Today* website, no date, http://www.historytoday.com/barbara-yorke/alfred-great most-perfect-man-history.

Books

B1 Anon, *Formule de Cérémonies et de Prières pour le Sacre de Leurs Majestés Impériales Napoléon Ier., Empereur des Français, et L'Impératrice Joséphine*, A Paris: Chez La Veuve Nyon, Année XIII, 1804.

B2 Anon, *The Arabic Gospel of the Infancy of the Saviour*, translated by Walker, A, in Ante-Nicene Fathers, Buffalo, NY: Christian Literature Publishing Co, 1886, revised and edited for New Advent by Kevin Knight, New Advent website, no date, http://www.newadvent.org/fathers/0806.htm.

B3 Appian of Alexandria, *Roman History*, translated by White, H, Loeb Classical Library, Cambridge, MA: Harvard University Press, 1912, 4 Volumes.

B4 Appian of Alexandria, *The Civil Wars*, translated by White, H, Loeb Classical Library, Cambridge, MA: Harvard University Press, London: William Heinemann Ltd, 1912.

B5 Asquith, C, *Shadowplay: The Hidden Beliefs and Coded Politics of William Shakespeare*, New York: Public Affairs, 2005.

B6 Bacon, F, *Considerations Touching a Warre with Spaine, 1624*, in *The Works of Francis Bacon, Baron of Verulam, Viscount St Alban and Lord High Chancellor of England*, London: Printed for A Millar, in the Strand, 1765, 5 Volumes, Volume 2, pp 299–319.

B7 Bainton, RH, *Here I Stand: A Life of Martin Luther*, New York and London: Meridian Books, 1995.

B8 Barbour, PL (Editor), *The Complete Works of Captain John Smith*, Chapel Hill: The Institute of Early American History and Culture/The University of North Carolina Press, 1969–1979, 3 Volumes.

B9 Barker, E, *Stories from the New Testament, for Children*, New York: Duffield and Company, 1911.

B10 Barrett, AA, *Caligula*, New Haven, CT: Yale University Press, 1990.

B11 Barrett, WP (Translator), *The Trial of Jeanne D'Arc: A Complete Translation of the Text of the Original Documents, with an Introduction*, London: Routledge & Sons, 1931.

B12 Belloc, H, *Charles I*, Norfolk, VA: Gates of Vienna Books, 2003.

B13 Berridge, K, *Madame Tussaud: A Life in Wax*, London: HarperCollins, 2007.

B14 Boulnois, L, *Silk Road: Monks, Warriors and Merchants on the Silk Road*, translated by Loveday, H, Hong Kong: Odyssey Books, 2004.

B15 Buchan, J, *Sir Walter Scott*, London: Cassell & Co; New York: Coward-McCann Inc., 1932.

B16 Budge, EAW, *The Literature of the Ancient Egyptians*, London: JM Dent and Sons, 1914.

B17 Calvino, I, *Invisible Cities*, translated by Weaver, W, London: Vintage Books, 1997.

B18 Cameron, E, *The European Reformation*, Oxford and New York: Oxford University Press, 2012.

B19 Carlyle, T, *Oliver Cromwell's Letters and Speeches: With Elucidations*, London: Chapman and Hall, 1850, 3 Volumes.

B20 Champlin, E, *Nero*, The Belknap Press of Harvard University Press, Cambridge, MA; London, England, 2003.

B21 Chapman, CE, *A History of Spain Founded on the Historia de España y de la Civilización Española of Rafael Altamira*, New York: The Free Press, London: Collier-Macmillan Ltd, 1965.

B22 Chapman, P, *The French Revolution as Seen by Madame Tussaud: Witness Extraordinary*, London: Quiller Press, 1989.

B23 Chifflet, JJ (Chifletio, JJ), *Anastasis Childerici I ...*, Antverpiae, Ex Officina Plantiniana: Balthasaris Moreti, 1655.

B24 Churchill, Sir WS, *My Early Life*, London: Butterworth, 1930.

B25 Cocceianus, CD [Cassius Dio], *Dio's Roman History*, translated by Cary, E, Loeb Classical Library, Cambridge, MA: Harvard University Press; London: William Heinemann Ltd, 1955, 9 Volumes.

B26 Cook, AS, *Asser's Life of King Alfred*, Boston, New York, Chicago, London: Ginn & Company, 1906.

B27 Cummins, J, *Francis Drake: The Lives of a Hero*, New York: St Martin's Press, 1997.

B28 d'Este, C, *Warlord: A Life of Winston Churchill at War*, New York: Harper Perennial, 2008.

B29 Davidson, MH, *Columbus Then and Now: A Life Reexamined*, Norman, OK: University of Oklahoma Press, 1997.

B30 De Barthe, J, *The Life and Adventures of Frank Grouard*, St Joseph, MO: Combe Printing Company, 1894.

B31 Dickens, C, *A Child's History of England*, London: Bradbury & Evans, 1852, 3 Volumes.

B32 Douglas, D, *The Journal of Sir Walter Scott from the Original Manuscript at Abbotsford*, New York: Harper and Brothers, 1891, 2 Volumes.

B33 Dusaulchoy, FN, *Historie du Couronnement ...*, A Paris: Chez PL Dubray ..., Thermidor Année 13, 1805.

B34 Epicurus, *Letter to Menoeceus*, in *Epicurus: The Extant Remains*, translated by Bailey, C, Oxford: The Clarendon

Press, 1926, pp 82–93.

B35 Eutropius, Roman History, translated by Watson, Rev JS, New York: Hinds & Noble, no date. Internet Archive website, no date https://archive.org/stream/eutropiusabridge00eutr#page/n39/mode/2up/search/nero.

B36 Flamarion, E, *Cleopatra: The Life and Death of a Pharaoh*, New York: Harry N. Abrams, 1997.

B37 Fletcher, J, *Cleopatra the Great: The Woman Behind the Legend*, New York: Harper, 2008.

B38 Ginzberg, L, *The Legends of the Jews*, Philadelphia: The Jewish Publication Society of America, 1913, 7 Volumes.

B39 Grossfeld, B, *The Targum Sheni to the Book of Esther: A Critical Edition Based on Ms. Sassoon 282 with Critical Apparatus*, New York: Sepher-Hermon Press, 1994–2002.

B40 Häberlein, M, *The Fuggers of Augsburg: Pursuing Wealth and Honor in Renaissance Germany*, Charlottesville, VA: University of Virginia Press, 2012.

B41 Haile, EW, *Jamestown Narratives: Eyewitness Accounts of the Virginia Colony*, Champlain, VA: RoundHouse, 1998.

B42 Hanford, F, *Did Betsey Ross Design the Flag of the United States of America?*, Publications of the Scottsville Literary Society, Number 7, Scottsville, NY: Isaac Van Hooser, 1917.

B43 Hasan-Rokem, G and Shulman, D (Editors), *Untying the Knot: On Riddles and Other Enigmatic Modes*, New York: Oxford University Press, 1996.

B44 Haw, S, *Marco Polo's China: A Venetian in the Realm of Khubilai Khan*, London: Routledge & Kegan Paul, 2006.

B45 Hawass, Z and Goddio, F, *Cleopatra: The Search for the Last Queen of Egypt*, Washington: The National Geographic Society, 2010.

B46 Herodotus, *Histories*, translated by Godley, AD, Loeb Classical Library, Cambridge, MA: Harvard University Press, London: William Heinemann Ltd, 1975, 4 Volumes.

B47 Hillerbrand, HJ, *The Reformation: A Narrative History Related by Contemporary Observers and Participants*, New York: Harper & Row, 1964.

B48 Hoose, P, *Claudette Colvin: Twice Toward Justice*, New York: Farrar Straus Giroux, 2009.

B49 Horace, *The Odes and Carmen Saeculare of Horace*, translated by Conington, J, London: George Bell and Sons, 1892.

B50 Hume of Godscroft, D, *The History of the House and Race of Douglas and Angus*, edited by Reid, D, Edinburgh: Scottish Text Society, 1992, 2 Volumes.

B51 Issaverdens, Rev Dr J, *The Uncanonical Writings of the Old Testament*, Armenian Monastery of St Lazarus, 1901.

B52 Italicus, S, *Punica*, translated by Duff, JD, Loeb Classical Library, London: William Heinemann Ltd, Cambridge, MA: Harvard University Press, 1961, 2 Volumes.

B53 Jacobs, CM, *Works of Martin Luther with Introductions and Notes*, Philadelphia: AJ Holman Co, 1915, 2 Volumes.

B54 James, L, *Churchill and Empire: Portrait of an Imperialist*, Weidenfeld and Nicolson, 2013.

B55 Jarvis, HW, *The Forgotten Adventure*, London: Pergamon, 1968.

B56 Jewel, L, *Keeper of the Ark: (A Moses Trilogy)*, Bloomington, IN: WestBow Press, 2012.

B57 Kelsey, H, *Sir Francis Drake: The Queen's Pirate*, New Haven, CT: Yale Nota Bene, Yale University Press, 2000.

B58 Kent, LA, *He Went With Marco Polo*, London: George G. Harrap & Co, 1936.

B59 Kluth, A, *Hannibal and Me: What History's Greatest Strategist Can Teach Us About Success and Failure*, New York: Riverhead Books, Penguin Group, 2011.

B60 Kneen, C, *Awake Mind, Open Heart: The Power of Courage and Dignity in Everyday Life*, New York: Marlowe & Company, 2009.

B61 Kraus, HP, *Sir Francis Drake: A Pictorial Biography*,

Amsterdam: N. Israel, 1970, on the Library of Congress website, Copyright 1970, http://www.loc.gov/rr/rarebook/catalog/drake/drake-home.html.

B62 LaPointe, E, *Sitting Bull: His Life and Legacy*, Layton, UT: Gibbs Smith, 2009.

B63 Littmann, Dr E, *The Legend of the Queen of Sheba in the Tradition of Axum*, Book 1 of *Bibliotheca Abessinica: Studies Concerning the Languages, Literature and History of Abyssinia*, Princeton, Leyden and The University Library: EJ Brill, 1904.

B64 Livy, *History of Rome*, translated by Foster, BO (Volumes 1–5), Moore, FG (Volumes 6–8), Sage, ET (Volumes 9–13), Loeb Classical Library, Cambridge, MA: Harvard University Press, London: William Heinemann Ltd, 1929, 13 Volumes.

B65 Lockhart, JG, *Memoirs of the Life of Sir Walter Scott, Bart*, Edinburgh: Robert Cadell; London: Whittaker & Co, 1837, 10 Volumes.

B66 Lodge, T, *Mandela: A Critical Life*, Oxford: Oxford University Press, 2006.

B67 Lucan, *Pharsalia*, in *Lucan: The Civil War*, translated by Duff, JD, Loeb Classical Library, Cambridge, MA: Harvard University Press, London: William Heinemann Ltd, 1962.

B68 Luther, M, *Preface to the Complete Edition of Luther's Latin Writings*, in Dillenberger, J, *Martin Luther: Selections from his writings*, New York: Anchor Books, 1962, pp 3–12.

B69 Maeterlinck, M, translated by Allinson, A, *The Massacre of the Innocents*, London: George Allen and Unwin, 1914.

B70 Maitland, FW, *The Constitutional History of England*, Cambridge: Cambridge University Press, 1908.

B71 Manchester, W and Reid, P, *The Last Lion Box Set: Winston Spencer Churchill, 1874–1965*, New York, Boston and London: Little, Brown and Company, 2012, 3 Volumes.

B72 Mandela, N, *Conversations with Myself*, Auckland: PQ Blackwell, 2010.

B73 Masson, F, *Napoleon and his Coronation*, translated by Cobb, F, Philadelphia & London: JB Lippincott & TF Unwin, 1911. French original published as *Le Sacre et le Couronnement de Napoléon*, Paris: Société d'Éditions Littéraires et Artistiques, 1908.

B74 McCabe, K, Roundtree, DJ, *Justice Older Than the Law: The Life of Dovey Johnson Roundtree*, Jackson, MS: The University Press of Mississippi, 2009.

B75 McCown, CC, *The Testament of Solomon: Edited from Manuscripts at Mount Athos*, Bologna, Holkham Hall, Jerusalem, London, Milan, Paris and Vienna, Leipzig: JC Hinrichs'sche Buchhandlung, 1922.

B76 McKechnie, WS, *Magna Carta: A Commentary on the Great Charter of King John with an Historical Introduction*, Glasgow: J. Maclehose, 1914 (2nd Edition, revised and in part re-written).

B77 McLaird, JD, *Calamity Jane: The Woman and the Legend*, Norman, OK: University of Oklahoma Press, 2012.

B78 Melancthon, P, *A History of the Life and Actions of the Very Reverend Dr Martin Luther, Faithfully Written by Philip Melancthon, Wittenberg, 1549*, in Fay, HJ, *Hymns of the Reformation by Dr Martin Luther …*, London: Charles Gilpin, 1845, pp 157–200.

B79 Moran, M, *Madame Tussaud*, London: Quercus, 2011.

B80 Mortimer, T, *The British Plutarch …* , edited and expanded by Wrangham, Rev F, London: Printed for J Mawman, Ludgate Street; and for Baldwin, Cradock and Joy, Paternoster Row, 1816.

B81 Mullett, MA, *The Catholic Reformation*, Abingdon and New York: Routledge, 1999.

B82 Murphy, AL, *Fifty Years of Challenges to the Colorline: Montgomery, Alabama*, History Thesis, Georgia State

University, 12 January 2009, http://scholarworks.gsu.edu/cgi/viewcontent.cgi?article=1036&context=history_theses.

B83 Musgrove, D, *100 Places That Made Britain*, London: BBC Books, 2011.

B84 Needham, J, *The Shorter Science and Civilisation in China*, Cambridge: Cambridge University Press, 1994.

B85 Nepos, C, *Life of Hannibal* in *Cornelius Nepos: Cornelii Nepotis Vitae adapted to the Hamiltonian System … for the use of Schools* by James Hamilton, Philadelphia: David McKay, no date.

B86 Ozment, S, *The Age of Reform: 1250–1550: An Intellectual and Religious History of Late Medieval and Reformation Europe*, New Haven, CT: Yale University Press, 1980.

B87 Parks, R with Haskins, J, *Rosa Parks: My Story*, New York: Dial Books, 1992.

B88 Parley, P, *Peter Parley's Book of Bible Stories, For Children and Youth, with Engravings*, Boston: Munroe & Francis, 1851.

B89 Parry, OR, *Betsy Ross and the United States Flag*, [publisher's details unknown], 1909.

B90 Philbrick, N, *The Last Stand: Custer, Sitting Bull, and the Battle of the Little Big Horn*, London: Vintage, 2011.

B91 Pipes, R, *The Russian Revolution*, New York: Knopf, 1990.

B92 Pliny the Younger, *Letters*, translated by Melmoth, W, revised by Hutchinson, WML, Loeb Classical Library, London: William Heinemann Ltd, 1931, 2 Volumes.

B93 Plutarch, *Lives*, translated by Perrin, B, Loeb Classical Library, Cambridge, MA: Harvard University Press, London: William Heinemann Ltd, 1967, 11 Volumes.

B94 Pollard, J, *Alfred the Great*, London: John Murray, 2005.

B95 Polo, M, *The Book of Ser Marco Polo the Venetian: Concerning the Kingdoms and Marvels of the East*, translated by Yule, Colonel H, London: John Murray, 1871, 2 Volumes.

B96 Polo, M, *The Description of the World*, translated by Moule,

AC and Pelliot, P, London: George Routledge & Sons Ltd, 1938.

B97 Polybius, *The Histories,* translated by Paton, WR, Loeb Classical Library, London: William Heinemann Ltd, New York: G. P. Putnam's and Sons, 2010, 6 Volumes; available on the LacusCurtius website, http://penelope.uchicago.edu/Thayer/E/Roman/Texts/Polybius/9*.html.

B98 Propertius, translated by Phillimore, JS, Oxford: At the Clarendon Press, 1906.

B99 Pseudo-Matthew, *The Gospel of Pseudo-Matthew,* edited by Roberts, A, Donaldson, Sir J, Coxe, AC, in Ante-Nicene Fathers, Buffalo, NY: Christian Literature Publishing Co, 1886, Volume 8, The Gnostic Society Library website, no date, http://www.gnosis.org/library/psudomat.htm.

B100 Radzinsky, E, *Rasputin: The Last Word,* London: Weidenfeld, 2000.

B101 Ramusio, GB, *Secondo Volume delle Navigationi et Viaggi...,* In Venetia: Nella Stamperia de Giunti, 1559.

B102 Rappaport, H, *Ekaterinburg: The Last Days of the Romanovs,* London: Windmill Books, 2009.

B103 Rawls, J, *A Theory of Justice,* Oxford: Oxford University Press, 1972.

B104 Reigart, Colonel JF, *The History of the First United States Flag,* Harrisburg, PA: Lane S. Hart, 1878.

B105 Reisner, Professor GA, *Mycerinus: The Temples of the Third Pyramid at Giza,* Cambridge, MA: Harvard University Press, 1931.

B106 Roberts, P, *Life and Death in Pompeii and Herculaneum,* London: British Museum Press, 2013.

B107 Robinson, JAG, *The Montgomery Bus Boycott and the Women Who Started It: The Memoir of Jo Ann Gibson Robinson,* edited with a foreword by Garrow, DJ, Knoxville, TN: The

University of Tennessee Press, 1987.

B108 Roger of Wendover, *Flowers of History*, translated by Giles, JA, London: Henry G. Bohn, 1849, 2 Volumes.

B109 Rose, J, *The Literary Churchill: Author, Reader, Actor*, New Haven and London: Yale University Press, 2014.

B110 Salmon, T, *A New Geographical and Historical Grammar ...* , Edinburgh, Printed by Sands, Murray and Cochran, for James Meuros, Bookseller in Kilmarnock, 1767.

B111 Sarfaty, DE, *Columbus Re-Discovered*, Pittsburgh: RoseDog Books, 2010.

B112 Saunders, CR and Chiplis, M, *For the Love of Letterpress: A Printing Handbook for Instructors and Students*, London: A&C Black Visual Arts, 2013. (www.letterpressluminaries.com).

B113 Schaff, D and Schaff, P, *History of the Christian Church*, New York: Charles Scribner's Sons, 1930, 8 Volumes. *Volume 5, Part 2: The Middle Ages – From Boniface VIII, 1294 to The Protestant Reformation* and *Volume 6: Modern Christianity – The German Reformation*.

B114 Schiff, S, *Cleopatra: A Life*, New York, Boston and London: Little, Brown and Company, 2010.

B115 Scott, Sir W, *Autobiography of Sir Walter Scott*, Philadelphia: Carey & Lea – Chestnut Street, 1831.

B116 Slater, W, *The Many Deaths of Tsar Nicholas II: Relics, Remains and the Romanovs*, London and New York: Routledge, 2007.

B117 Steinberg, MD, and Khrustalëv, VM, *The Fall of the Romanovs: Political Dreams and Personal Struggles in a Time of Revolution*, New Haven and London: Yale University Press, 1995.

B118 Stevenson, WH, *Asser's Life of King Alfred, Together with the Annals of St Neots Erroneously Ascribed to Asser*, Oxford: Clarendon Press, 1904.

B119 Strabo, *Geography*, translated by Jones, HL, Loeb Classical Library, Cambridge, MA: Harvard University Press,

London: William Heinemann Ltd, 1967, 8 Volumes.

B120 Strydom, L, *Rivonia Unmasked,* Johannesburg: Voortrekkerpers, no date.

B121 Suetonius, *The Lives of the Caesars,* translated by Rolfe, JC, Loeb Classical Library, Cambridge, MA: Harvard University Press, London: William Heinemann Ltd, 1979, 2 Volumes.

B122 Tacitus, *Annals,* in *Complete Works of Tacitus,* edited by Church, AJ; Brodribb, WJ and Bryant, S, New York: Random House Inc., 1942.

B123 Tanner, JR, *Tudor Constitutional Documents A.D. 1485–1603 with an historical commentary,* Cambridge: At the University Press, 1922.

B124 Telberg, GG, and Wilton, R, *The Last Days of the Romanovs,* New York: George H. Doran & Co, 1920.

B125 Thacher, JB, *Christopher Columbus: His Life, His Work, His Remains …,* New York and London: G. P. Putnam's Sons, 1903, 3 Volumes (in 6 parts with 5 pamphlets).

B126 Thompson, EM, *Understanding Russia: The Holy Fool in Russian Culture,* Lanham, MD: University Press of America, 1987.

B127 Thornbury, W, *The Royal Palace of Westminster in Old and New London,* London, Paris & New York: Cassell, Petter & Galpin, 6 Volumes, Volume 3, pp 491–502; the British History Online website, November 2013, http://www.british-history.ac.uk/report.aspx?compid=45170.

B128 Trench, RC, *The Star of the Wise Men: A Commentary on the Second Chapter of St. Matthew,* London: John W. Parker, 1850.

B129 Tussaud, JT, *The Romance of Madame Tussaud's,* London: Odhams Press Limited, 1921.

B130 Tussaud, Madame [M], *Memoirs and Reminiscences of the French Revolution,* edited by Hervé, F, 2 Volumes,

Philadelphia: Lea & Blanchard, 1839. Volume I is on the Google Books website, http://books.google.co.uk/books?id=EVYqAAAAYAAJ.

B131 Tyldesley, J, *Cleopatra: Last Queen of Egypt*, New York: Basic Books, 2008.

B132 Utley, RM, *The Lance and the Shield: The Life and Times of Sitting Bull*, New York: Ballantine Books, 1993.

B133 Victor, Sextus Aurelius, Book 3, Lines 11–12 of *The Caesars* (*De Caesaribus*) translated by Bird, HW, Translated Texts for Historians, Liverpool: Liverpool University Press, 1994.

B134 Vincent, Bishop JH, *Herod Sends His Soldiers to Kill the Little Boys who Lived in Bethlehem*, in *My Mother's Bible Stories, Told in the Language of a Gentle, Loving Mother Conversing with her Children*, Philadelphia, PA and St Louis, MO: People's Publishing Company, 1896, pp 315–317.

B135 Virgil, *Aeneid*, in *Virgil*, translated by Fairclough, HR, revised by Goold, GP, Loeb Classical Library, Cambridge, MA; London, England: Harvard University Press, 2000, Volumes 1, 2.

B136 Vogel, HU, *Marco Polo Was in China: New Evidence from Currencies, Salts and Revenues*, Leiden, Boston and Tokyo: Brill Publishing, 2012.

B137 Vyse, Colonel H, *Operations Carried on at the Pyramids of Gizeh in 1837*, London: James Fraser, 1840, 2 Volumes.

B138 Wade, J, *British History, Chronologically Arranged …*, London: Effingham Wilson, Royal Exchange, 1839.

B139 (Wairy, L) Constant, *Recollections of the private life of Napoleon*, translated by Clark, W, Akron, Ohio: The Saalfield Publishing Company, 1907, 3 Volumes.

B140 Wallace, Prof PG, *The Long European Reformation: Religion, Political Conflict, and the Search for Conformity, 1350–1750*, Hampshire and New York: Palgrave MacMillan, 2004.

B141 Weaver, AG, *The Story of Our Flag, Colonial and National*, Chicago: AG Weaver, 1898.

B142 West, JA, *Serpent in the Sky: The High Wisdom of Ancient Egypt*, Wheaton, Madras and London: Quest Books, 1993.

B143 Whitelocke, B, *Memorials of the English Affairs from the Beginning of the Reign of Charles the First to the Happy Restoration of King Charles the Second*, Oxford: At the University Press, 1853, 4 Volumes.

B144 Whitford, DM (Editor), *Reformation and Early Modern Europe: A Guide to Research*, Sixteenth Century Essays & Studies 79, Kirksville, MI: Truman State University Press, 2008.

B145 Wilder, T, *The Ides of March*, New York: Perennial, 2003.

B146 Winterling, A, *Caligula: A Biography*, translated by Schneider, DL; Most, GW and Psoinos, P, Berkeley, Los Angeles, London: University of California Press, 2011.

B147 Wood, F, *Did Marco Polo Go to China?*, Colorado: Westview Press, 1996.

B148 Woolf, R, *The English Mystery Plays*, Berkeley and Los Angeles: Unversity of California Press, 1980.

B149 Woolley, RM, *Coronation Rites*, Cambridge: Cambridge University Press, 1915.

Online resources

C1 *A Map of Siberia showing the Trans-Siberian Railway from Perm to Vladivostok dated 1903* can be found at Parovoz: The Site about Railways of Russia, C.I.S. and the Baltics, 1995–2012,
http://www.parovoz.com/maps/transsib.jpg.

C2 Addison, P, *Paul Addison's top 10 books on Churchill, The Guardian* website, Monday, 11 April 2005,
http://www.theguardian.com/books/2005/apr/11/top10s.churchill.

C3 Alexander II, *The Abolition of Serfdom in Russia: The Manifesto of February 19, 1861* (English translation – translator unknown), Documents in Russian History on the

Seton Hall University website, 10 February 2009, http://academic.shu.edu/russianhistory/index.php/Alexander_II%2C_Emancipation_Manifesto%2C_1861.

C4 Anon, *A Fresh Case of "Generational Chauvinism"*, The Churchill Centre website, Press Release, 18 April (2008), http://www.winstonchurchill.org/learn/in-the-media/churchill-in-the-news/530-a-fresh-case-of-qgenerational-chauvinismq.

C5 Anon, *Dig 'may reveal' Cleopatra's tomb*, BBC News website, Wednesday, 15 April 2009, http://news.bbc.co.uk/1/hi/world/middle_east/8000978.stm.

C6 Anon, *Russia's last tsar rehabilitated*, BBC News website, Wednesday, 1 October 2008, http://news.bbc.co.uk/1/hi/world/europe/7645776.stm.

C7 Anon, *Saakashvili Testifies Before War Commission*, Civil Georgia website, 28 November 2008, http://www.civil.ge/eng/article.php?id=20043.

C8 Anon, *Sainthood for last tsar*, BBC News website, Monday, 14 August 2000, http://news.bbc.co.uk/1/hi/world/europe/880205.stm.

C9 Anon, *Sharpeville Massacre – 21 March 1960*, South African History Online (SAHO) website, no date, http://www.sahistory.org.za/topic/sharpeville-massacre-21-march-1960.

C10 Anon, *St Stephen's Chapel 1184–1363*, UK Parliament website, no date, http://www.parliament.uk/about/living-heritage/building/palace/estatehistory/the-middle-ages/early-chapel-st-stephen.

C11 Anon, *St Stephen's Hall*, UK Parliament website, no date, http://www.parliament.uk/about/living-heritage/building/palace/architecture/palace-s-interiors/st-stephen-s-hall.

C12 *Archaeological Areas of Pompei, Herculaneum and Torre*

Annunziata, UNESCO website, World Heritage List, date of inscription 1997,
http://whc.unesco.org/en/list/829.

C13 Barnes, KJ, *Lucille Times*, in the *Montgomery Advertiser*, on The Montgomery Bus Boycott website, no date,
http://www.montgomeryboycott.com/lucille-times.

C14 Bethancourt III, WJ, *Witch Hunt*, The Internet Sacred Text Archive, 1990–2001,
http://www.sacred-texts.com/pag/burning.htm.

C15 Bracton [or Bratton], H de, *De legibus et consuetudinibus Angliae, Bracton on the Laws and Customs of England*, translated by Thorne, SE, Cambridge, MA: The Belknap Press of Harvard University Press, in association with the Selden Society, 1968, Harvard Law School Library website, 1998,
http://bracton.law.harvard.edu.
Table of contents available at
http://bracton.law.harvard.edu/Unframed/calendar.htm.
Sections relevant to the monarchy can be found at
http://bracton.law.harvard.edu/Unframed/English/v2/19.htm#TITLE1,
and at
http://bracton.law.harvard.edu/Unframed/English/v2/33.htm#TITLE38.

C16 *Brown v. Board of Education of Topeka – 347 U.S. 483 (1954)*, Justia website, US Supreme Court records, no date,
http://supreme.justia.com/cases/federal/us/347/483/case.html.

C17 Bruegel [the Elder], P, *Massacre of the Innocents*, 1565–7, Royal Collection Trust website, 2014,
http://www.royalcollection.org.uk/collection/405787/massacre-of-the-innocents.

C18 Carlson, M, *Witches and Witchtrials in France*, Marc Carlson's Homepage, University of Tulsa website, 1998/2000, http://www.personal.utulsa.edu/~marc-carlson/witchtrial/france.html.

C19 Churchill, W, *"Never give in": Speech given at Harrow school on 29 October 1941*, The Churchill Centre website, no date, http://www.winstonchurchill.org/learn/speeches/speeches-of-winston-churchill/103-never-give-in.

C20 Clark, LD, *Teaching with Documents: Sioux Treaty of 1868*, The US National Archives and Records Administration website, no date, http://www.archives.gov/education/lessons/sioux-treaty/#documents.

C21 *Criminal Court Case No. 253/1963 (State Versus N Mandela and Others)*, United Nations Educational, Scientific and Cultural Organization (UNESCO) website, submitted in 2007, http://www.unesco.org/new/en/communication-and-information/flagship-project-activities/memory-of-the-world/register/full-list-of-registered-heritage/registered-heritage-page-2/criminal-court-case-no-2531963-state-versus-n-mandela-and-others/.

C22 Crow, C and Corr, S, *First Impressions: Rude Britannia, History Today* magazine blog, Wednesday, 9 June 2010, http://historytodaymagazine.blogspot.co.uk/2010/06/first-impressions-rude-britannia.html.

C23 Cruikshank, G, *The Corsican Shuttlecock*, 10 April 1814, Wikimedia website, 3 August 2005, http://commons.wikimedia.org/wiki/File:Cruikshank_-_The_Corsican_Shuttlecock.png.

C24 David, J-L, *Napoleon Crossing the Alps*, 1802/3, Wikimedia, 10 February 2012, http://commons.wikimedia.org/wiki/File:Jacques-Louis_David_008.jpg.

C25 de Courteille, AP, *Mirâdj-nâmeh: récit de l'ascension de Mahomet au ciel …*, Paris: Ernest Leroux Éditeur, 1882,

Internet Archive website, no date,
https://archive.org/stream/mirdjnmehpublip00navogoog#page/n8/mode/2up.

C26 Delaroche, P, *Napoleon Crossing the Alps*, 1850, Wikimedia, 19 July 2012,
http://commons.wikimedia.org/wiki/File:Paul_Delaroche_-_Napoleon_Crossing_the_Alps_-_Google_Art_Project_2.jpg.

C27 *Ex Parte Troy University – 961 So.2d 105 (2006)*, Justia website, Alabama Supreme Court Decisions, no date,
http://law.justia.com/cases/alabama/supreme-court/2006/1051318-9.html.

C28 *Eyes on the Prize Interviews: Transcript of Interview with Rosa Parks*, 14 November 1985, Washington University in St Louis Digital Gateway website, 2004,
http://digital.wustl.edu/cgi/t/text/text-idx?c=eop;cc=eop;rgn=main;view=text;idno=par0015.0895.080.

C29 Fendel, H, *Holy Ark Announcement Due on Friday*, Israel National News website, 25 June 2009,
http://www.israelnationalnews.com/News/News.aspx/132067#.UwpCYWJ_uSo.

C30 Foxe, J, *The Unabridged Acts and Monuments Online* or TAMO (1570 edition), HRI Online Publications, Sheffield, 2011,
http://www.johnfoxe.org.

C31 Fraser, C, *Egypt's great pyramids 'not built by slaves'*, BBC News website, Monday, 11 January 2010
http://news.bbc.co.uk/1/hi/world/middle_east/8453026.stm.

C32 Fraser, M (Translator), *Napoleon's concordat (1801): text*, Concordat Watch website, no date,
http://www.concordatwatch.eu/showkb.php?org_id=867&kb_header_id=826&order=kb_rank%20ASC&kb_id=1496.

C33 Hartwig, JP, *Jakob Fugger and his Influence on the*

Reformation, Middler Church History, 30 December 1980, Wisconsin Lutheran Seminary Library website, no date, http://www.wlsessays.net/files/HartwigFuggerInfluence.pdf.

C34 Hawass, Z, *The Discovery of the Tombs of the Pyramid Builders at Giza*, Guardian's Egypt website, 1997, http://guardians.net/hawass/buildtomb.htm.

C35 Hicks, P, *Napoleon's Consecration and Coronation*, Fondation Napoléon website, no date, http://www.napoleon.org/en/reading_room/articles/files/482285.asp.

C36 Hole, W (engraver), *Map of Virginia, discovered and as described by Captain John Smith, 1606*, Wikimedia website, 17 March 2011, http://commons.wikimedia.org/wiki/File:Virginia_map_1606.jpg.

C37 Hunt, Dr P, *Hannibal in the Alps: Stanford Alpine Archaeology Project 1994–2006*, Archaeolog Blog, 2006, http://traumwerk.stanford.edu/archaeolog/2006/04/hannibal_in_the_alps_stanford_1.html.

C38 *Illustration of a piece of cast metal type*, Wikimedia, 23 March 2011, http://commons.wikimedia.org/wiki/File:Metal_type.svg.

C39 *In Re Estate of Rosa Louise Parks*, Justia website, Michigan Court of Appeals – Unpublished Decisions, 2009, http://law.justia.com/cases/michigan/court-of-appeals-unpublished/2009/20090319-c281203-88-281203-opn.html.

C40 Joan of Arc bibliography, *Jeanne d'arc la pucelle* website, no date, http://www.jeanne-darc.info/p_multimedia_literature/0_bibliography_list.html.

C41 Kluth, A, *Hannibal and Me blog*, at http://andreaskluth.org/blog/.

C42 Langworth, RM, *Now for Something Completely Different*,

Review of Ratnu, ID, *Layman's Questions About Churchill*, Jaipur, India: Mumal Publishers, 1998, The Churchill Centre website, no date, http://www.winstonchurchill.org/component/content/article/12-learn/261-laymans-questions-about-churchill.

C43 Lentz, T, *Napoleon and Charlemagne*, Fondation Napoléon website, no date, http://www.napoleon.org/en/reading_room/articles/files/lentz_charlemagne.asp.

C44 Lienhard, JH, *Napoleon's Ariel Crown*, Engines of Our Ingenuity, Episode 2404, University of Huston website, no date, http://www.uh.edu/engines/epi2404.htm.

C45 *Life and death in Pompeii and Herculaneum*, British Museum website, 2013, http://www.britishmuseum.org/whats_on/past_exhibitions/2013/pompeii_and_herculaneum.aspx.

C46 Livy, *Periochae*, in Latin and English, Livius website, no date, http://www.livius.org/li-ln/livy/periochae/periochae00.html.

C47 Luther, M, *Letter to the Archbishop of Mainz, 1517*, on the Fordham University Website, Medieval Sourcebook, 1996, http://www.fordham.edu/Halsall/source/lutherltr-indulgences.asp.

C48 MacRae, G, *The Apocalypse of Adam*, The Gnosis Archive website, 1990, http://www.gnosis.org/naghamm/adam.html.

C49 Macrobius, *Saturnalia*, available on the LacusCurtius website, 13 October 2006, http://penelope.uchicago.edu/Thayer/L/Roman/Texts/Macrobius/Saturnalia/1*.html.

C50 Mandela, N, *Freedom in our Lifetime*, 30 June 1956, on the ANC website, no date, http://www.anc.org.za/show.php?id=2603.

C51 Mandela, N, *I am prepared to die: Nelson Mandela's statement from the dock at the opening of the defence case in the Rivonia Trial*, Monday, 20 April 1964, Nelson Mandela Centre of Memory website, http://db.nelsonmandela.org/speeches/pub_view.asp?pg=item&ItemID=NMS010&txtstr=prepared%20to%20die.

C52 Manuscrit Français 5524 de la Bibliothèque Nationale de Paris – Folio 142, illustrated in *Coat of Arms: Family arms and nobility*, on the Jeanne d'arc la pucelle website, no date, http://www.jeanne-darc.info/p_jeanne/coat_of_arms.html.

C53 *Morgan v. Virginia – 328 U.S. 373 (1946)*, Justia website, US Supreme Court records, no date, http://supreme.justia.com/us/328/373/case.html.

C54 Morné, JK, *Rivonia Trial: 50 Years Later*, Jacaranda FM website, 22 November 2013, http://www.jacarandafm.com/post/rivonia-trial-50-years-later.

C55 *Native Tribes of Britain*, BBC History website, 2014, http://www.bbc.co.uk/history/ancient/british_prehistory/iron_01.shtml#twentyfour.

C56 O'Malley, F and Degliobizzi, M, *Rethinking Rosa Parks*, Delaware Social Studies Education Project: Teaching American History Workshop, 12 March 2011, University of Delaware website, no date, http://www.dcte.udel.edu/hlp2/resources/civilrights/Lesson-Rethinking_Rosa_Parks.pdf.

C57 Parks, R, *Merv Griffin Show Interview*, 1983, YouTube, 26 June 2012, http://www.youtube.com/watch?v=L3h6s9jxZtE.

C58 Perks, R, *Rescuing the Rivonia Trial recordings*, British Library website, 6 December 2013, http://britishlibrary.typepad.co.uk/sound-and-vision/2013/12/rescuing-the-rivonia-trial-recordings.html.

C59 Pleasant, Flt Lt T, *A History of the School of Fighter Control*, The Association of Royal Air Force Fighter Control Officers website, 1990–2014, http://www.raffca.org.uk/sfc03woodlands.html.

C60 Police Department, Montgomery, *Police Report for Claudette Colvin, 3/2/55*, facsimile of arrest report, The Martin Luther King, Jr. Research and Education Institute website, no date, http://mlk-kpp01.stanford.edu:5801/transcription/document_images/InVol6/550302-001.pdf.

C61 Police Department, Montgomery, *Rosa Parks' Arrest Records*, Internet Archive website, 13 November 2012, https://archive.org/stream/514415-rosa-parks-arrest-records#page/n3/mode/2up.

C62 *Records relating to the 'Treason Trial' (Regina vs F. Adams and Others on Charge of High Treason, etc.), 1956 1961*, AD1812, Historical Papers, The Library, University of the Witwatersrand, Johannesburg, South Africa, May 2012, Historical Papers archive website, WITS Library website, http://www.historicalpapers.wits.ac.za/?inventory/U/collections&c=AD1812/R.

C63 Rees, C, *Pyrrhic Victory: The Disputation at Pleissenburg Castle*, the website of Christopher Rees, 1996–2003, http://www.reesnet.com/theology/luther/.

C64 Reni, G, *Massacre of the Innocents*, 1611, Wikimedia website, 25 May 2013, http://commons.wikimedia.org/wiki/File:Guido_Reni_-_Massacre_of_the_Innocents.jpg.

C65 Rubens, PP, *Massacre of the Innocents*, 1611/12, Art Gallery of Ontario website, no date, http://www.ago.net/agoid106855.

C66 Rubens, PP, *Massacre of the Innocents*, WGA20259, *c.* 1637, Wikimedia website, 26 November 2013, http://commons.wikimedia.org/wiki/File:Peter_Paul_

Rubens_-_Massacre_of_the_Innocents_-_WGA20259.jpg.

C67 *Rosa Parks 1913–2005: We Air a Rare 1956 Interview with Parks during the Montgomery Bus Boycott*, Democracy Now! Tuesday, 25 October 2005, Internet Archive website, no date, https://archive.org/details/dn2005-1025_vid. The interview starts around 12 minutes in.

C68 Schroeder, C, *Politics on the Half Shell: Caligula's seashells revisited*, 143rd Paper Abstracts of the 143rd Annual Meeting of The American Philological Association (APA), 5–8 January 2012, APA website, Last modified 19 September 2013, http://apaclassics.org/annual-meeting/572schroeder.

C69 Shaw, D, *Quest for Cleopatra's Tomb Reveals Statue*, BBC News website, Sunday, 9 May 2010, http://news.bbc.co.uk/1/hi/world/africa/8670557.stm.

C70 *Stèle commémorative de Coco …*, Wikimedia website, 23 April 2014, http://commons.wikimedia.org/wiki/File:St%C3%A8le_comm%C3%A9morative_de_Coco,_dernier_chien_de_Marie-Antoinette.jpg.

C71 *Sweatt v. Painter – 339 U.S. 629 (1950)*, Justia website, US Supreme Court records, no date, https://supreme.justia.com/cases/federal/us/339/629/case.html.

C72 *The Freedom Charter as adopted at the Congress of the People, Kliptown, on 26 June 1955*, on the ANC website, no date, http://www.anc.org.za/show.php?id=72.

C73 The Montgomery Improvement Association, *Integrated Bus Suggestions*, 19 December 1956, Inez Jessie Baskin Papers, Alabama Department of Archives and History website, last updated 10 December 2013, http://www.archives.state.al.us/teacher/rights/lesson1/doc7.html.

C74 *The Mystery of Marie Antoinette's Beloved Dog "Coco"*, Matthew Fraser's website, 1 September 2013, http://www.matthewfraserauthor.com/history/the-mystery -of-marie-antoinettes-beloved-dog-coco.

C75 *The Walter Scott Digital Archive,* Edinburgh University Library website, no date, http://www.walterscott.lib.ed.ac.uk/home.html.

C76 Thomas, B, Construction of the Giza Pyramids, World-Mysteries website, 2005, http://www.world-mysteries.com/gw_tb_gp.htm.

C77 *Timeline,* Nelson Mandela Foundation website, 2014, http://www.nelsonmandela.org/content/page/timeline.

C78 *Transcript for the trial of Rosa Parks vs. City of Montgomery,* Alabama Department of Archives and History, 15 September 2009, http://digital.archives.alabama.gov/cdm/ref/collection/voices/id/2100.

C79 *Tributes,* Nelson Mandela Centre of Memory website, 2012, http://db.nelsonmandela.org/tributes/pub_view.asp?pg=search1&opt=guided.

C80 *United Nations General Assembly Resolution 1761,* United Nations General Assembly website, 6 November 1962, http://www.un.org/documents/ga/res/17/ares17.htm.

C81 *United States v. Sioux Nation of Indians – 448 U.S. 371 (1980),* Justia website, US Supreme Court records, no date, http://supreme.justia.com/cases/federal/us/448/371/case.html.

C82 Various, *Famous People Who Hear Voices,* Intervoice: The International Hearing Voices Network website, 2014, http://www.intervoiceonline.org/about-voices/famous-people.

C83 Various, *Sort (typesetting),* Wikipedia, 10 January 2014, http://en.wikipedia.org/wiki/Sort_(typesetting).

Resources for further exploration

Brigham Young University – Harold B. Lee Library – Euro Docs website
http://eudocs.lib.byu.edu/index.php/Main_Page
Online Sources for European History – Selected Transcriptions, Facsimiles and Translations.

British History Online
http://www.british-history.ac.uk/
A digital library containing some of the core printed primary and secondary sources for the medieval and modern history of the British Isles. Created by the Institute of Historical Research and the History of Parliament Trust, it aims to support academic and personal users around the world in their learning, teaching and research.

The British Library
http://www.bl.uk/

CELT Corpus of Electronic Texts
http://www.ucc.ie/celt/
The Free Digital Humanities Resource for Irish history, literature and politics.

Constitution Society – Citizen Action website
http://constitution.org/cs_civic.htm
The Constitution Society is a private non-profit organization founded in 1994 and dedicated to research and public education on the principles of constitutional republican government. It publishes documentation, engages in litigation, and organizes local citizens groups to work for reform.

EdTech Teacher – Best of History websites
http://www.besthistorysites.net/index.php/
An award-winning portal that contains annotated links to over 1,200 history websites as well as links to hundreds of quality K–12 history lesson plans, history teacher guides, history activities, history games, history quizzes, and more. Recommended by The Chronicle of Higher Education, the National Council for the Social Studies, the New York Public Library, the BBC, Princeton University, among others.

Fordham University's Internet History Sourcebooks Project
http://www.fordham.edu/Halsall/index.asp
The Internet History Sourcebooks Project is a collection of public domain and copy-permitted historical texts presented cleanly (without advertising or excessive layout) for educational use.

History Matters website
http://historymatters.gmu.edu/
A US-centric annotated collection of websites organized by theme, with information classified according to category (Archive, Electronic Essay, Gateway, Journal, Organization, Syllabi/Assignments) and type of resource (text, images, audio, and video).

History Today Magazine
http://www.historytoday.com/
First published in 1951, the magazine continues to provide up-to-date, well-researched, general articles on historical topics for the general reader which are reliable and well edited.

Infomine – Scholarly Internet Resource Collections
http://infomine.ucr.edu/
A resource hosted by the University of California, a joint venture with several US colleges, it contains useful Internet resources

such as databases, electronic journals, electronic books, bulletin boards, mailing lists, online library card catalogues, articles, directories of researchers, and many other types of information.

The Institute of Historical Research
http://www.history.ac.uk/
One of ten member Institutes of the School of Advanced Study, part of the University of London, it provides a gateway to a large number of resources for historians and researchers.

The Internet Archive
https://archive.org/
The Internet Archive, a 501(c)(3) non-profit, provides a digital library of Internet sites and other cultural artefacts in digital form, providing free access to researchers, historians, scholars, the print disabled, and the general public.

The National Archives
http://www.nationalarchives.gov.uk/
The official archive and publisher for the UK government, and for England and Wales.

Online Library of Liberty
http://oll.libertyfund.org/
A collection of scholarly works about individual liberty and free markets.

University of Cambridge, Anglo-Saxon, Norse & Celtic Department
http://www.asnc.cam.ac.uk/resources
Various sections can be accessed by clicking on the 'Resources' tab on the navigation bar.

The US Library of Congress website
http://www.loc.gov/

Virgo – University of Virginia Library
http://search.lib.virginia.edu/catalog
A selection, including digital resources, of the library's holdings.

Forthcoming titles in the Treasure Trove series of Cultural Riddles

Art Riddles

Over 25 well-known scenes from the history of art presented as riddles suitable for use with Odyssey boards. Each riddle is presented with an enticing title, a set of clues, a detailed historical essay outlining the facts and context in which the events take place. A list of cross-curricular activities that could lead out from an exploration of the subject is also available.

Bedlam

There's something strange about this room. It seems to be suffused with a buttery-yellow light that's generated by the furniture in it. There's not much furniture, though… a table, with a bottle of water, a drinking glass, a ceramic basin and ewer, and some clear glass bottles in a box; two chairs; a bed; a hook and a hanging rail for clothes. That's it. Oh – and the pictures – the pictures on the walls. Many of them are hanging at very odd angles. It's rather a small room, if you ask me – you'd be hard-pressed to fit more than a couple of beds in it. A typical bachelor's room, or a solitary painter's. The paintings on the walls are probably by the artist – two of them could be portraits of friends or acquaintances – one might possibly even be a self-portrait.
There are a couple of doors – one on each of the side walls – but they're both closed. The window in the back wall is ajar… are those yellow shutters beyond it, or the intensity of the sunlight on a clear summer's day? Everything seems to point back into the enclosed space of the room itself.

Within that space, the whole painting seems to be moving. Lines of perspective never quite meet up – they veer away from their vanishing points whenever they intersect with another offset line, as if constantly beckoning you, the viewer, into the heart of the room, inviting you to try out the bed, sit on the chair, reach over to the table and pour some water into the glass, open the window, breathe in the air, the smell of paint... and wonder... are you in the painting, or an artist's bedroom? And if you looked out of the window, what might you really see, hear, feel... beyond the surface of the canvas we call reality...?

Clues

1. The specific painting in this riddle dates from 1888.
2. The artist painted three version of this particular painting.
3. The artist considered this painting to be one of his best paintings.

Riddles from Classical Music

Over 25 well-known scenes from the world of classical music presented as riddles suitable for use with Odyssey boards. Each riddle is presented with an enticing title, a set of clues, a detailed historical essay outlining the facts and context in which the events take place. A list of cross-curricular activities that could lead out from an exploration of the subject is also available.

Ouch!

A handsome man, dressed in a long velvet frock coat, with silk embroidery, over tunic and breeches, stockinged legs and shoes that matched his coat, ornamented with silver buckles, is standing in front of an orchestra in the hall of mirrors at Versailles, in a long flowing wig of curls. He's conducting a small orchestra of superb musicians – the best in the country in a piece of music he's composed to celebrate his patron's recovery from illness. In his mind, he's conducting a ritual. He's recreating and rebalancing the music of the spheres, for he sees himself as one of the satellites which revolve around their patron, their central sun. He beats time using a device like a long walking stick. At a particularly dramatic cadence, he accidentally hits his foot. It's painful, but he doesn't cry out.

Who is this man? Who is his patron? Where are they and when? What happens to the conductor as a result and why?

Clues

1. The musician started out as a dancer and loved composing ballets for his patron, who particularly enjoyed dancing.
2. The musician is credited with the invention of the French style of opera known as Lyric Tragedy (Tragédie Lyrique).
3. The musician was the friend of the French playwright, Molière, with whom he collaborated on several occasions.
4. The patron was known as The Sun King.
5. The patron was the fourteenth person to adopt the name of Louis.

Further titles in the Treasure Trove Series of Cultural Riddles

Bible Riddles
Science Riddles
Literature Riddles
Maths Riddles
Popular Music Riddles
Architecture Riddles
Geography Riddles
Riddles from Myths and Legends
Riddles from Children's Literature
Riddles from the World of the Moving Image

Liberalis is a Latin word which evokes ideas of freedom, liberality, generosity of spirit, dignity, honour, books, the liberal arts education tradition and the work of the Greek grammarian and storyteller Antonius Liberalis. We seek to combine all these interlinked aspects in the books we publish.

We bring classical ways of thinking and learning in touch with traditional storytelling and the latest thinking in terms of educational research and pedagogy in an approach that combines the best of the old with the best of the new.

As classical education publishers, our books are designed to appeal to readers across the globe who are interested in expanding their minds in the quest of knowledge. We cater for primary, secondary and higher education markets, homeschoolers, parents and members of the general public who have a love of ongoing learning.

If you have a proposal that you think would be of interest to Liberalis, submit your inquiry in the first instance via the website: www.liberalisbooks.com.